N·I·N·E
V·I·S·I·O·N·S

N·I·N·E V·I·S·I·O·N·S

A Book of Fantasies

Andrea LaSonde Melrose,
EDITOR

THE SEABURY PRESS • NEW YORK

For Rondo

dearest friend and companion,
who adventures with me,
understanding sometimes—
laughing often—
loving always.

1983
The Seabury Press
815 Second Avenue
New York, N.Y. 10017

Library of Congress Cataloging in Publication Data
Main entry under title:

Nine visions, a book of fantasies.

1. Fantastic fiction, American.   I. Melrose, Andrea LaSonde.
PS648.F3N56   1983   813'.0876'08   83-8967
ISBN 0-8164-2490-X

"Someone to Watch Over Me" © 1983 by Hilary Andrewes.

"Unworthy of the Angel" © 1983 by Stephen Donaldson.

"Certain Distant Suns" from *High Crimes and Misdemeanors* by Joanne
Greenberg. Copyright © 1977, 1979 by Joanne Greenberg. Reprinted by
permission of Holt, Rinehart and Winston, Publishers.

"Pursuit of a Lost Tugolith: a tale of Pelmen before the
dragon was divided" © 1983 by Robert Don Hughes.

"Vocation" © 1983 by Katherine Kurtz.

"The One Hundred and First Miracle" © 1983 by Crosswicks, Ltd.

"Ceyx" © 1983 by Starr Luteri.

"The Aqueduct" © 1983 by Calvin Miller.

"Mother and the Flying Saucer" © 1976 by Mary McDermott Shideler.
Originally published by Pegana Press.

Contents

· *Acknowledgments* ·

I owe a debt of gratitude greater than I can express to the following people:

> my mother, who taught me to read, and my father, who willingly supported what came to be a very expensive habit;

> the authors who contributed to this anthology, every one of whom found time for personal notes of advice and enthusiasm when I needed buoying up, every one of whom was prompt and cheerful about revisions, delays, and problems, and every one of whom has my undying respect, admiration, and affection;

> and Robert Unger, who saw me through the practical things.

INTRODUCTION

This book is a collection of religious fantasies. Because I believe that what is finest in fantasy speaks not to any specific group of people, but to people of all traditions and backgrounds, this anthology is not meant to be exclusive in any way. I want people from all walks of life to be able to pick up these stories and find in them challenge and hope and wonder and love; I want no one to be excluded. As I have thought about it, however, it seemed to be a good idea to share what I mean by the term "religious fantasy."

Theologically, there is a great difference between an icon and an idol. The first is an open window; the second, a brick wall. An icon is something which points beyond itself; it can be seen through; it is in one sense a lens. It is a symbol of something other and greater than what it appears to be. To work, an icon must have some element of the familiar. Something totally alien will not serve because there is no way for the eye and heart to go through it and beyond it; the outward image is too arresting. For this reason, extremely strict rules govern the painting of religious icons. It is of prime importance that the art, the image, not call attention to itself: its purpose is to act as a focus. If the eye stops at the image itself, the object is in danger of becoming an idol.

Icons are not limited to our religious life; they are all around us. They tend to be associated with what is highest and most noble because, in serving as a focus, they point us outward into the infinite and eternal. To me, the most important aspect of fantasy is this aspect of symbolism. The story must be filled with icons and must itself be an icon. As such, it cannot reasonably be pulled apart and analyzed because the component parts somehow equal more than their sum. Because an icon is a lens, a focus, what it points to will be slightly different for each person.

It is not really necessary to understand what an icon is to have the icon work. To use a familiar example, Aslan in C.S. Lewis' Narnia books is an icon not only because he is a symbol but because, like the woodshed on the the hill in *The Last Battle,* he is bigger on the inside than he is on the outside. It is the rare child who fails to recognize Aslan as a symbol; he is not only a lion, or the Son of the Emperor Beyond the Sea, he represents a type of behavior and relationship, he calls forth questions about one's own being. He points not only to what he symbolizes, but to our *connection* with what that symbol stands for. How we respond as individuals depends on who we are.

In using the Narnia books as an example, I am not implying that fantasy must of necessity deal with mythical beasts or imaginary worlds. But fantasy must contain the element of symbolism, of iconography, and it must be sufficiently startling to catapult us into using the icon. The "startle" isn't enough in itself, any more than the icon is enough alone—they must be connected in such a way that when we startle, we look instinctively toward the icon to help us understand the point.

C.G. Jung's work on archetypes is particularly helpful in understanding fantasy because fantasy, like fairy tales, in dealing with icons, deals with archetypes. As human beings we feel a need for connectedness. On some instinctive and basic level we reach out continually to find common ground, common experiences, ways to relate to one another. One of the most frightening and troubling aspects of our twentieth-century society is a seemingly voluntary alienation. We cut ourselves off from one another with tape recorders and headphones turned high to block out the sounds of the city—and the sounds of other human voices. We spend hours in front of television sets living vicariously. Yes, those each have their benefits, but in all honesty how often do we use the "benefits" as justification for separating ourselves from others?

The increasing interest in Jung and fantasy and fairy tales is, perhaps, a tentative turn in the tide. It is a way of saying, "We are part of a race—the human race. We have common memories and common icons. There are certain symbols, certain characters, which evoke common response." It is a way of saying, "I belong."

The stories in this anthology come from many different pens; they come from people who have little in common except a passionate belief in symbol and pattern. You can see that belief shining through every one of the pieces in this book. There is a reason for what happens to us, a reason that has to do with our interconnectedness. We are not independent in the sense of being unconnected. In each of these stories there is a feeling of obligation, of duty.

"Duty" is a particularly slippery word in this age of self-expression and the individual. It has come to imply a commitment imposed on one from outside the self. But a far clearer definition is found in Robert Heinlein's *Time Enough For Love.*

> Do not confuse "duty" with what other people expect of you; they are utterly different. Duty is a debt you owe to yourself to fulfill obligations that you have assumed voluntarily. Paying that debt can entail anything from years of patient work to instant willingness to die. Difficult it may be, but the reward is self-respect.

It is this sense of duty that appears in every one of these stories. Duty is one of the most consistent icons in all fantasy.

Children who read fantasy, who have fought alongside the Pevensies and the Narnians in *The Last Battle,* or have followed Irene and Curdie through the goblin caves, will never lack for courage. Courage is not the absence of fear, as someone much wiser than I once said. Courage is accepting fear and facing it; it is pushing at the horizons and the limits. It is being willing to confront the fear long enough to name it, for it is the unnamed fear that has the most power. To name a fear is not to eliminate it, but to be able to handle it.

In fantasy we all—readers and characters—face mysteries and fears . . . and in the facing we allow parts of ourselves which have lain dormant to surface. We find ourselves realizing that our deepest fears can be faced. We find common experiences through the icons and archetypes, experiences we can translate and apply to our daily lives. We find friends, and heroes, and teachers who call us to higher achievements and nobler visions.

Finally, in true fantasy, no individual accomplishes alone. What is done is done in the context of community, or the context of the sacrifice of other individuals, or in connectedness to a strong and positive power outside ourselves. It is here that religious fantasy differs most strongly from any other form of literature: religious fantasy always involves a relationship to a power outside ourselves—to the Other. And that power, whatever we may call it, does not accomplish alone, either; it does not act, cannot act, apart from the creatures of the universe of the fantasy.

Fantasy calls us to our vocation . . . a vocation in relationship to a love and power apart from the self. I call that power God, you may call it the Divine, the Eternal Essence, the Transcendent; it is all one. It calls us to leave behind the broken parts of what we were yesterday and grow toward wholeness and maturity. What is religious fantasy? It is that part of the literature which tries to help us, through icon and commitment and relationship, to see "face to face." It tries to catch, however fleetingly, a clear vision of the truth and it offers it in the only language in which truth can be clothed—the language of symbol and archetype, the language which connects.

Calvin Miller

"The Aqueduct" is a particular joy to read, not only because it is a treasure for Miller fans, but because it is the only piece in the anthology which qualifies as a love story in the usual meaning of that term. It is in the simple, straightforward love of Nardia and Tintellie that we find one of the most powerful icons in the story. Their love sits, jewel-like, in the midst of a wealth of symbol; its very gentleness is startling. Just as real power can be totally tender, so a powerful icon can be of the utmost simplicity.

Their sacrifice reminds us that life is a continual dying. We must always be willing to lay aside our life so that something greater can come in its place. On an intimate scale we are called to do this every day: to let go of the self which is living at this moment and to move toward a stronger, truer self. It is a continual diving into the unknown, a continual reaching toward the ultimate.

As we move forward in that eternal searching and growing which are such an intrinsic part of the human story, I am reminded that love is not only the goal, but love provides the impulse and the guidance. Dame Julian of Norwich put it beautifully over 500 years ago:

> Do you want to understand your Lord's meaning in this experience? Understand it well: love was his meaning. Who showed it to you? Love. What did he show you? Love. Why did he show it? For Love.

· Calvin Miller ·

THE AQUEDUCT

The Aegean island of Roos was the scene of my lonely vigil after the others were gone. I had packed the tools knowing that Dethios would come early in the morning to load the last of the equipment and close the excavation site permanently. Tonight I would be the only living human being on the island. As I nailed shut the last crate of tools, I realized that my hope when I had come to Roos was to take back crates, not of tools, but of artifacts. I felt unfulfilled.

I cannot say the dig had been completely fruitless, for I had learned the folly of basing archaeology on hearsay and legend. The natives of the nearby islands had rehearsed for a millennium the myth of a huge aqueduct in which fresh water could have followed a lofty channel across the ocean inlets of brine 300 feet beneath it. Our digging, however, uncovered not even a hint of any foundation stones for such an aqueduct.

I had also learned the error of high-risk gambling. If the natives had been right about the aqueduct, I would have become a well-known archaeologist. Instead, I had used up two years of my life and was bankrupt—the financial endowment of my sponsors gone. I had hoped to prove that certain primitive forms of Greek architecture had originated among Sanskrit-speaking natives of the Eastern Mediterranean twelve hundred years before Homer. Most serious archaeologists considered my theory a pipe dream, since aqueducts like those at Segovia, Spain, were unknown before the expansive projects of the Roman architects. My melancholy deepened as I contemplated the opportunities my peers would take to point out my folly.

I was disconsolate and alone.

This night on Roos the tide was high, the hollow roar of the water against the black rocks only adding to my depression. In the late afternoon light, I picked my way along the well-worn path, past the site of the excavation to a lonely pinnacle of land where I could observe the grey Aegean and feel the cold sting of the winds for the last time. I sat and thought of the past of Greece and the early Aegean—a glory and civilization now gone.

A gull shrilled behind me, calling my attention to the rain moving in from the sea. The streaks in the distant sky resembled fractures upon the horizon and the slate grey waters breaking in white foam on the wet stones sent my imagination back to a day when sea-maids called to the land creatures on the high rocks, begging them to dive to their deaths.

Bound as I was by the grey mist and the sea, the raucous call of the gull behind me shocked me into leaping to my feet. I turned and saw it, perched on a rock, head cocked to watch me, beak open as it called again. It had interrupted my reverie and self-pity. Not wanting to be bothered, I picked up a loose piece of rock and tossed it close to the gull—expecting the bird to fly away. Instead, it moved closer and repeated its shriek.

Intrigued, I darted toward the gull, waving my arms, but it only moved out of reach, continuing to call. I followed, childishly annoyed by its persistence. It would move a few feet and shriek impudently; I would follow, waving my arms and shouting back. In this way we moved off the pinnacle of land and further along the path from the excavation. Finally the bird stopped. This time as I made my lunge, it rose squawking on its wings and, wheeling, sailed away. As I stood panting I felt drops of rain. The storm had moved in while I played my idiotic game with the gull and I realized that with the rain had come nightfall. I turned back the way I had come, hoping to make shelter before the downpour. In the dim light, I tripped and fell forward, my upper torso trembling extended over the brink of a precipice. The white cascades of the ocean roared and frothed like churning hell below me. In the split second before I eased my way back from the edge, I thought I caught a glimpse of a cave mouth. Glancing carefully over the brink again, I saw a small ledge only two feet below me.

This part of the island was not unfamiliar to me. I knew of the rocky and precipitous inlet into which I had all but fallen, but no one had discovered or explored the cave below. This seemed an ideal time to make a cursory examination, as the cave would provide shelter from the storm.

Lowering myself cautiously over the edge, I felt for and found the ledge with my foot. It seemed sturdy and I gradually allowed my weight to rest on it. When there was no ominous shifting, I inched forward and found the cave mouth. Within, it was dry and I sat just under the overhang, gazing out at the falling rain.

Time passed and gradually the storm abated. Now I waited for moonrise to provide the light for me to clamber back onto the path and find my way back to my tent in the deserted camp. Slowly the clouds cleared and the sky filled with the glint of new evening stars. Orion, thrice-studded at his galactic belt and sword point, was lying down on the horizon. The full moon leaped into the sky and spread its cool light into the cave where I sat. The rain and stars had washed away some of my misery and I began to look with interest around my temporary refuge. As I watched the cave thus revealed, the moon rose higher and I found myself star-ing at an iron chest sitting against the back wall. I moved across the cave and laid eager hands on the lid. Childish memories of *Treasure Island* supplied the chest with jewels from Spanish galleons and pieces-of-eight.

It was at this point that the cryptic words engraved on the box caught my attention. They were in ancient Greek and read, "Our gift to the coming King." My mind soared. Here, indeed, was an ancient treasure box—someone's gift to a reigning monarch. Fe-verishly I searched for the bolts, praying that they could be broken open with a rock at hand. To my surprise, they slid apart with the ease of newness. Throwing open the lid I confronted not treasure—only a jumble of bones. The chest was filled with them. There were two skulls lying on top of the collection; as one was slightly larger than the other, I guessed that one was a man's, the other a woman's. I was baffled. Had I found some strange form of burial urn?

Judging more from the Greek inscription on the top of the chest than from the appearance of the bones themselves, I felt that they probably dated to the time of Christ. The skulls seemed to grin at me in a kind of triumph. I laid their leering visages at some distance from each other and in the moonlight began to examine and separate the rest of the bones.

As time passed, I realized that I was coming upon a growing collection of bones that did not seem to be human at all. The weeks of exhausting work excavating, and the dullness of the task at hand, began to take their toll: slowly my eyes began to ache, and through my fatigue it seemed that the bones themselves began to glow. Without realizing it, I gradually slipped into an uneasy, dream-filled slumber.

In the shallows of the still night sea I walked through thick mists out of which rose a triple-arched aqueduct. Through its lofty trough, I could hear the clean water gurgling down from the highlands while at my feet there lapped the harsh sound of ocean waves. I pushed forward through the green mists, on toward the inlet of the sea. Suddenly, I could hear two people engaged in soft conversation. Moving forward, I caught sight of them.

A woman was seated on a rock a foot from the shore, fluttering her naked feet in the water—kicking at it and stirring it, splashing lightly in the small Aegean waves. A man was turned toward her, talking and laughing as he sat on a broad log on the shore. I was immediately embarrassed, for they were both naked and their gentle voices bespoke intimacy.

In the slow motion of my dream world, I moved back into the shadows of the cliff face. The conversation rippled like the lilt of a ballad played sweetly on a balalaika.

The man spoke. "I have lamented all my life my terror of the sea."

"But why, Tintellie?" And the woman laughed—a shimmering tumble of sound. "Sea is but a gathering of water, and only water of the very kind that fills the moutain lakes where you were born."

"Only water, it is true. But the sea lies low, Nardia. Change your mind; come with me to the high meadows."

"I cannot leave the sea! All life was born here, Tintellie. Leave your tree-wrapped mountains and your granite heights and settle here. Come dwell with me."

At this he turned and gazed back toward the land. "Nardia . . . never can our marriage be; we're both too much afraid: you of the heights and I of the sea. You were born here among these sea-washed stones, the sound of the wild surf pounding in your ears while Neptune chained you to himself."

There was a pause and then the woman answered, something new in her voice. "Neptune, Tintellie. Can Neptune *be?*"

"As sure as there is sea. He rides a leathery kraken with his trident raised. His being cleaves the deep and all his towering sovereignty presides above the sea."

"I've been here at these waters since the day that I was born. I've heard the hollow tide roar perpetually. But never yet have I seen Neptune break the sea. There is no Neptune, Tintellie! No Zeus or Hera either. . . . I've lived so long and waited for the gods to stir the waters of the sea. They never came. The sea is at peace by night or noon—the gulls, not the gods, preside. The gulls are free; they pay not the slightest heed to dead Neptune. Why should they, Tintellie, for he is Not. Neptune only lives in marble statues made by men who never understood the seagulls' language. I tell you, Tintellie, I'll not believe in Neptune till the gulls do."

"I beg you, Nardia, do not blaspheme."

"Oh, Tintellie, the gulls do not lie. Have you ever on the heights of your bold meadow sky seen any of the gods?"

The man sat silent, refusing to answer her. She spoke again.

"Listen, love, your silence says it all. You've never seen them either. I cannot say from where they came—perhaps from the minds of men who'd rather invent deities than dare to live without them. Still," and here she paused again and then resumed with stronger voice, "there is strange music in the skies above us now. I heard a gull scream the other day; a gull who, soaked in lather from a distant flight, split the bold aurora and cried away the night."

"What did this winged-thing say?"

"He said, 'Look higher than Olympus! There is a world above the shallow mountain—and in that world there is but one God, who has forsaken all his starry realms to touch the lands Olympus couldn't change.' Neptune indeed! He never was . . . or he is dead. We were too slow to learn that God is always One. Now we know the lie of Mount Olympus and, knowing, we concede Medusa tamed, the kraken killed, the griffins gone. He is come and he is One and the times of gods and trolls are done."

"I cannot bear to think our age is gone, or that strong Olympus' peak is leveled. You've learned too much; believed too radically. Now we have little hope of living, and our love, once separated by the sea, cannot much longer be. Tell me while you splash these shoals, do you not lament that your believing controls and chains your life? I tell you, Nardia, I cry that Neptune is gone and centaurs die and mermaids live in bondage without souls." He leaned forward over the edge of the water and kissed her hair and neck. She returned the kiss, pain and sorrow written in her eyes. "The time is short! Come leave the sea and fly with me to the high and rocky cliffs of my secluded home."

"I turned my back on what cannot be. I left the gods and now I leave the sea. And think, my love, it's all illusion: Zeus never Was and neither, dear, were we. We but existed where the minds of men could conjure up our forms. I'm glad they carved our statues just before we took our leave of history."

"Oh, Nardia, never to have Been: a heavy price, but noble if it grants that God may reign in deeper realms of reality. Come, my love, we'll grieve the nothingness which gives to humanity its destiny."

So saying, the man rose. I was surprised that in the darkness I had thought him sitting on a log. In truth his lower torso folded neatly into the body of a horse. He reached his powerfully muscled arms and caught Nardia. The woman I had thought was sitting on a rock, had for her lower half the body of a fish. Holding her close, he turned.

"Nardia, what did the gulls say he was like—this one who'd conquered new lands?"

"They said he'd come from God to set his love in human form."

He carried her up the beach and galloped past me, stirring the green mist. His gold hooves clicked on the paving near the aqueduct before he disappeared. A moment later, they reappeared on a pinnacle above the aqueduct and they kissed. Then they turned briefly to face the grey sea and the east, and I heard them singing as one:

> *What are our paltry lives*
> *What pittance is our hope to be,*
> *If by our joyous going we may call him forth*
> *Who makes one of both earth and sea?*
> *I love you, Nardia.*
> *I love you, Tintellie.*

Robert Hughes

I read the first of Robert Hughes' fantasies, *The Prophet of Lamath,* at a time in my life when I, like Pelmen in that book and in this story, was searching for the Power. I was in the midst of personal crisis, feeling deserted and alone; I turned thirty and, on my birthday, my dearly-loved grandfather died. During the few days following his death, I spent a lot of time mourning and remembering and as I began to heal I was able to recall many times I had felt deserted in the past, only to discover months later that far from being alone, I was being upheld and supported by the love of family and friends. . .even by the charity (which in its purest form is love) of strangers.

We stumble blindly on our way, often running (as Pelmen is) from a responsibility we are afraid to take on, from a burden we don't think we can carry. We thrash and flail, certain that we are drowning, panicked, as if unreasoning activity were going to help us. Somehow, into that darkness, comes a moment of peace when a friend gives us a hug, a stranger reaches out a hand . . . and we realize that we have been standing on a rock all along: supported, stable, safe. However we see that gesture—as God working through the human beings around us or simply as the generosity of the human spirit coming through the day-to-day masks we all wear—the gift is infinitely precious. Like many of the important lessons in life, it is something which must be learned many times. There are days when we remind ourselves of the tugolith, plunging straight ahead, trampling everything in our path, driven by something or someone we cannot even name. And then, like sunlight or the warmth of a friendly fire, will come other days when we recognize the Power—however we name it—always there, always reaching out, always loving . . . bearing us.

· Robert Don Hughes ·

PURSUIT OF A LOST TUGOLITH
A Tale of Pelmen Before the Dragon Was Divided

Pelmen stood upon the roadway, gazing in surprise at the absolute obliteration of a stone cottage. It was autumn, and the ground was covered with red and gold leaves—not tornado season at all. Yet it was clear this had happened recently, for though the clearing was ringed with brightly colored trees, few falling leaves had found their way into what had been the hut's interior. With the chill wind that had blown throughout the morning, it seemed unlikely that would be the case unless this accident had just occurred. But what could have caused such massive destruction so quickly?

"It was a tugolith that did this," muttered a voice beside him, startling Pelmen and causing him to wheel around with a jerk. The man gazed forlornly at the wreckage, then pulled his brown cloak tightly around his shoulders and sighed.

"Are you the owner?" Pelmen asked.

"Of what?"

"Of this cottage."

"No," the man sighed again. "Of the tugolith."

Now Pelmen had often heard of tugoliths, but he'd never seen one. He was fascinated. "Did he escape?" he asked.

"Tugoliths don't really escape, as such," the man replied. "They usually just wander off, like a toddler at a picnic. Most of them are not very good at directions, so someone always has to chase after them. Few people are thoughtful enough to bring a lost tug back."

Pelmen gazed at the destroyed building and thought he could understand why. "Are you sure it's your animal who did this?"

"Certainly. His name's Evanlitha, and I've been following him all morning."

"Humph," Pelmen grunted. "He certainly did an effective job of demolishing this cottage."

"You think this is bad? You should see what he did to a whole village back that way." The tugolith handler pointed back across the road and into the trees. As Pelmen turned to look, he could easily see the path the beast had made for himself through the underbrush. Fallen trees and broken shrubs marked it clearly.

"What had the village done to cause your beast to go on such a rampage?"

The man shrugged. "It got in his way. It's hard to teach a tug to go around something he could just as easily go through." Pelmen raised his eyebrow in response. "By the way," the man went on, "if you will, call him by his name—Evanlitha. He's sensitive, and if he hears someone call him a beast he gets offended."

Pelmen nodded thankfully and filed that bit of information for future reference. There was no creature he knew of that was larger or more powerful than a tugolith, save the dragon himself. It didn't seem healthy to offend something that big. "Evanlitha," he repeated, and the handler nodded. "And what is your name— if you don't mind my asking?"

The handler looked at him sharply, and seemed to think this over carefully before replying; there was good reason. The garment Pelmen wore was a pale, sky blue—the habitual vestment of the Divisionist order of the Dragonfaith. All of the people of this northern section of Lamath were Dragonfaithers—that is, they believed in the lordship of Vicia-Heinox, the two-headed dragon that lived at the center of the world. But the great majority of these were orthodox Coalescents. They regarded Divisionists as heretics. Pelmen's robe advertised not only that he was a Divisionist, but a Divisionist monastic as well. Pelmen wasn't surprised when the tugolith handler hesitated. "I guess it won't matter if you know. I'm Dresher the tugoman, from some distance south of here. And you?"

"I'm Pelmen," the blue-robed brother replied. He gave no further description of himself, though he might have. He could have added, "the player," for that was what he was called in Chaomonous. More impressively, he could have termed himself "the powershaper," for in the magical land of Ngandib-Mar he was highly regarded as a wizard. But here, in the cold northlands of Lamath on the very edge of winter, he chose to be known only as a wandering monk.

"You're a long way from your people, aren't you?" Dresher observed.

"Am I?" He said it as vaguely as he could. He didn't want the conversation to center on himself.

"Why, yes. Aren't most Divisionists in the South?"

"They may be," Pelmen nodded, sounding uninterested.

"What are you doing 'way up here then?"

"Oh, maybe the same thing your tugolith is doing."

"What's that?"

"Just going forward—and waiting for someone to come and herd me back to where I ought to be." He said this in an offhanded manner calculated to encourage Dresher to think again about his animal. In fact, there was much truth in what Pelmen said. It really was the way he felt.

"Who's going to do that?"

"My keeper," Pelmen shrugged. Then he pointed. "Would Evanlitha have gone that way?"

"Straight ahead," Dresher replied wearily. "That's one good

thing about chasing a tug—they don't turn off to right or left . . . and they leave you a clearly marked trail!"

"So it appears," Pelmen smiled. "Shall we follow it?"

"You want to go with me?" Dresher asked.

"Why not?"

"Well—you're—you're a religionist. A priest or something. I figured you'd have better things to do."

"Nothing comes to mind."

Dresher looked this stranger over carefully, noting the gaunt face and the high cheekbones. Mostly he noticed Pelmen's eyes, which were piercing—the same blue as his gown. Instinctively Dresher knew this was a man with charisma—a man who would attract attention whether he sought it or not. And in this region, with that color robe, such attention would likely be dangerous. Nevertheless, Dresher liked him and a man who handled tugoliths rarely needed to fear the bodily attack of other men. "Certainly," he nodded, and he smiled. "I'd be glad to have you join me." And so, Pelmen and Dresher left the road, in search of a lost tugolith.

It took only a couple of hours to catch up with him. Evidently, Evanlitha's morning stroll had made him hungry, and he'd lingered long enough to devour the entire contents of a barn some miles beyond the ruined cottage. They found a farmer next to the devastated barn, pulling on his hair and cursing. The man had little hair to pull. Perhaps his baldness reflected his response to previous frustrations.

"Ah, Pelmen?" Dresher muttered, "I realize, you being a cleric and all, that you're probably pretty given to honesty. But just for the moment, would you mind not saying anything to this farmer about my connection with Evanlitha? I mean, I'll come back later on and settle up with him, of course."

Pelmen shrugged. He was used to people having sudden fits of honesty in his presence, and didn't seem to mind having that effect. The two men tried to walk on past the former barn without being seen, but Pelmen's robe was rather brilliant in color. When the farmer caught sight of it he stopped pulling his straggly mane and stared. Then ever so slightly, his frown deepened.

Dresher noted that expression just before they walked out of sight, and it worried him. It was clear that the man had reacted much more sharply to Pelmen's robe than to his concern over his ruined barn. And that was bad. When a farmer thinks more about his religion than he does about his hay supply, something's been going on in that community. Dresher picked up speed, and Pelmen adjusted his stride to suit. Pelmen, too, had noticed the farmer's look. He wasn't surprised.

Soon they left the forest, and Dresher's worries about the community's reaction to Pelmen were eclipsed by his concern for Evanlitha. Above them rose a high, rocky ridge, crowned with a picturesque village. A cobbled road wound up the hill, small stone cottages lining it on either side, all the way to the top. And on the summit, its twin spires topped with huge effigies of the dragon's heads, was the local Dragonfaith chapel. It was this hill Evanlitha was endeavoring to climb, but he wasn't using the road, he was going straight up one side. Naturally, he wasn't making very fast progress. He had, however, already torn up one thatched-roof cottage and a couple of gardens, and a number of white-haired little old ladies were telling him what they thought about it. From a distance, of course.

Dresher broke into a run, and Pelmen quickly followed. They chose to take the road, and soon had raced up to where the cluster of women stood shouting and shaking their fists. As Dresher dashed through and around them, several of them began demanding, "Is that your monster?" When it became clear that it was, they heaped abuse on him. When Pelmen joined him, however, they hushed. The light blue tint of his robe elicited shocked silence.

Pelmen was used to such treatment from Coalescents. He ignored them, and caught up to Dresher in time to hear the handler ask Evanlitha, "What are you doing?" The man used the voice one might when addressing a small child.

Evanlitha didn't look at him, but kept pressing upward as he said, "I'm going up."

"I can see you're going up, Evanlitha. Can you tell me why?"

"Must go up," the enormous beast murmured, and with a thrust of his horn and a toss of his head he knocked another obstacle out of his path. A moment before it had been an attractive wall. Now it was a scattering of rocks.

"But why, sweetheart?" Dresher asked. He didn't scold, he only pleaded.

"Don't know," the tug grunted. He strained to force his massive forequarters through the hole he'd made in the wall. He made it through. The hole, however, was enlarged in the process.

"If you don't know *why*, are you sure you must?" Dresher asked sensibly.

Evanlitha didn't hesitate. "Sure I must."

"Who told you you must?" Dresher winced as he said it. That horn had just pulled back, preparing to plunge through the wall of yet another cottage.

"Don't know," Evanlitha answered. Then there was a crash, and another shower of stones bounced down the hillside.

"If you don't know who told you, how do you know you should?" Dresher pleaded, a bit frantically.

"I *know*," Evanlitha grumbled.

"Is it possible that you're going up without a reason?"

"Got a reason," said the tugolith, as the other side of the cottage came tumbling down.

"Who gave you the reason!" Dresher shouted, his temper starting to slip.

"I must," Evanlitha called, as he knocked another wall aside. The tugolith was now on a higher level of the hill. Dresher and Pelmen quickly started around the hill, following the road, to catch up with him again.

Dresher noticed Pelmen's slight smile, and snapped, "What's funny?"

"Oh, I'm just thinking that Evanlitha reminds me of myself."

"Yourself? How?"

"I plunge blindly ahead, oblivious to where I'm going or why, or who I might be injuring in my progress. And I wonder: Is my handler talking to me with the same patience you have? Am I just not able to hear?"

"Who's your handler?" Dresher grunted.

"The Power."

"Who's that? Lord Dragon?"

"No. The Power has nothing to do with the two-headed dragon."

"But I thought you believed in the dragon! You're wearing Divisionist blue."

"There are Divisionists and Divisionists. I have no wish to worship a man-eating serpent. I'm a Divisionist not because I view the world dualistically and think the dragon's two heads represent the forces of good and evil; I'm a Divisionist because I think the entire beast is evil, and want to see him divided *permanently*." By this time they had rounded the hill back to Evanlitha's side, and something Pelmen had said had caught the tugolith's attention.

Pelmen looked up to see the tugolith's enormous eyes regarding him dolefully. "You call me beast?" he asked. He seemed hurt.

"Not you, Evanlitha. I spoke of Vicia-Heinox."

That evidently settled the matter. Evanlitha wheeled back around and started again up the mountain. Pelmen looked back at Dresher, and saw the man peering at him as if he were a venomous snake. After a moment, the handler spoke. "You're a heretic."

Pelmen looked down at the cobbled street, and said quietly, "You know, there are problems with a label like that. If you use it about me, I'll probably be tempted to use it about you. Pretty soon it'll end up not meaning much of anything at all."

"But you don't believe in the dragon! You don't believe in any of our traditions!"

"You're right. Traditions in themselves don't mean very much to me. And it's only by tradition that anyone would worship that particular dragon! If you ever talked to him you'd discover he's a stupid, greedy monster. I'm talking about the dragon, Evanlitha!" Pelmen called, for at the term "monster" the tugolith had hesitated and cast a glance over his shoulder. "I worship the one who met me when I sought Him. I call Him the Power, but what's in a name? He *is*. And He loves me. And He's not a dragon."

Dresher stared at Pelmen, his lip curled in distaste. Then he shook his head, as if attempting to throw off the effects of such heretical notions. "Well. I'm not one to comment on a man's religion. That's what we pay priests and priestesses for, right? To set us straight?"

"Is it?" asked Pelmen. By his expression he made it clear that he thought otherwise.

"It's not my business," Dresher grunted. "But listen, Pelmen, you're in danger. Maybe you don't know it, but there's been a priestess going through these parts lately, name of Serphimera! She's been stirring up people all over, telling them they ought to go down to Dragonsgate and let the Lord eat them! Doesn't make much sense to me, but a lot of people are taken with her, and by the way these people are eyeing you, I'm afraid she's been through here!"

Pelmen had long been aware of the unfriendly eyes fixed upon him from every direction. "I think you're probably right," he said, and almost added "my friend." For Dresher's sake, he thought better of it.

"Then run!" Dresher whispered with intensity. "If anybody overheard you speaking, they'll kill you!"

"Dresher," Pelmen whispered back, "I'm in the middle of their town. You think if I tried to run now I could get away from them?"

Dresher shook his head, staring at Pelmen as if he thought him mad. "If you knew that, why did you come here?"

Pelmen again examined the cobblestones. "I don't know," he said. Then he chuckled, reminded by his own words of the tugolith's stolid replies. "Maybe I've come to be killed. Maybe I've come to learn something more about the Power. Or maybe—"

and here he frowned, "maybe I've been running away. I found a book recently—an old book—that seems to place an enormous burden on someone's shoulders, if I've interpreted it rightly. Maybe I'm running away because I don't want to be the one to bear that burden." He smiled a bit to think he was making this confession to a tugolith handler. On the other hand, who could really understand? Certainly not the priests of the dragon. They were so busy being proprietors of the truth that they hadn't time to listen to truths from anyone else.

"I don't think you'll have to bear any burden," Dresher murmured, his eyes on the chapel above them. "I don't think you'll live long enough." What had been a low murmur suddenly burst into a roar. From the doors of the chapel gushed a flood of Dragonfaithers in dark blue robes—midnight blue, the color of Coalescents. And from the sound of their clamor, they were enraged. Dresher was swept aside as the mob boiled down around the twisting road toward Pelmen.

Pelmen held his ground, waiting. Had he glanced behind him, he would have seen that other villagers had walled off his escape route. Some of them scowled up at him in wrath. Others grinned, eager for what was to come.

Many hands grabbed him—none gently. He was quickly bound, and hustled up the curving street at a trot, the cries of pious bloodlust ringing in his ears. He got a glimpse of the countryside from the steps of the chapel: it was lovely, the trees vying with one another to produce the most striking reds and oranges. Then they whirled him around and shoved him through the double doors. His head snapped back and he caught sight of those dual, dragon-headed spires. It seemed the enormous painted eyes peered down at him with a vengeful glee. Then he was inside.

The interior of the chapel glowed with diffused blue light, which streamed in through windows of stained glass. He was manhandled to the front of the structure, then hurled forward by a half-dozen hands to crash into a plastered wall. With his hands bound, he had no way to break his fall and his head split on the stone. He rolled onto his back in pain, eyes clenched shut. Then they opened, and he saw above him yet another image of the ubiquitous dragon. Its two heads smiled down on him hungrily. He heard a chorus of rasping noises, and realized it came from knives being drawn from their sheaths. He felt no fear at that moment, nor any elation either—only a sense of puzzlement, and maybe some relief that, after all, he was not the one who would have to bear the burden. Then he heard the chanting. Though his thoughts were fuzzy from the blow to his head, he recognized it immediately: "I believe in the dragon, may he preserve us. May he hold the stars and earth together in tension. May he hold good and evil together in tension. May he hold my interests and his interests together in tension, until such a time . . . ."

There was a rumbling. The chant faded out, and the blue-clad figures with their drawn knives began to look nervously around their sanctuary. The terracotta statue of Vicia-Heinox began rocking on its base, and it was as if the dragon's heads were weaving before them, mesmerizing them in preparation for consumption. Then with a rumble and a crash, the statue toppled forward, and the dark blue robes flapped as the Dragonfaithers raced out the doors in fear just as they had earlier raced out in rage. Pelmen looked up to see it falling on him, and closed his eyes, ready to absorb the final shock.

He felt an impact. But nothing that broke his neck, or crushed him. He opened his eyes again.

Above him loomed Evanlitha's enormous horn. And to either side of him lay the broken remains of the statue—one head in pieces to his right, the other to his left. "Evanlitha!" he cried. "Thank you!"

"What for?" asked the huge animal.

"You saved my life."

"Yes," the tugolith nodded.

"But . . . why?" Pelmen asked.

The tugolith breathed an exasperated sigh. "I must!" he snorted.

"But . . . who told you to?" Pelmen said. He spoke the words rather quietly, and waited expectantly for the reply.

The gigantic animal only shrugged. "I don't know," he said. But Pelmen did.

Dresher stepped through the huge opening Evanlitha had made in the front of the chapel. "Evanlitha," he groaned, "how could you—Pelmen?"

Pelmen smiled up at him. Then things began to appear blurred, and he sank back into the rubble of the statue.

Pelmen rode the tugolith's horn down the curving road through the village. Evanlitha seemed to feel no more compulsion to go straight. Having saved Pelmen, he was willing to be led. And for their part, none of the villagers felt inclined to get in the great tug's way. Nor did Dresher stop when they got to the bottom of the hill, but led his huge charge home with Pelmen still riding on Evanlitha's head. There he put Pelmen to bed, and finally the wandering monastic got the sleep his body craved.

The next day Pelmen felt much better, and rose early to leave. Dresher met him at the door. "I think," he began, "you may have to bear that burden after all."

Pelmen smiled. "Perhaps so, my friend. But now I'm sure of something I wasn't certain of before."

"What's that?"

"That there's already someone bearing me."

Hilary Andrewes

Courage and obedience are intricately connected and that connection is, for me what this story is all about. We often think of courage as spectacular action against overwhelming odds, but cannot courage also be obedience to one's calling through easy times and hard? Obedience is accepting the call when it comes, whether we feel ready or not. And, as Elek tells Polyhistor in this story, we are never truly ready. We are always asked to struggle with our imperfections, with our weaknesses, with our unreasoning fears. Obedience is always a choice; we have the right to say "No." Courage is what helps us say "Yes" when our heart is pumping madly, the adrenaline is pouring into our system, and everything inside is screaming, "No!"

I love this particular story because Andrewes does very little of the work for us; she demands that we use our imaginations; she demands that we co-create. Co-creation is a topic that almost every author in this book has addressed at some point in his or her writings. One of my seminary professors has suggested that co-creation is the vocation of every human being; it is a statement of our connectedness to the universe, to the power that sets the stars ablaze, that causes the iris to bloom each spring, that patterns the strands of DNA in each cell. When Polyhistor answers her call, she is doing what each of us does in a different way with every breath we take.

Obedience is a way of living; it frees us to be that which we are called to be, it frees us to co-create. When we find or are given the courage to say "Yes" to what has been asked of us, we are able to channel our energy in creative and powerful ways. Obedience is not blindness; it is not to be confused with putting the responsibility for our actions on someone else's shoulders. It is taking on the duty which is ours and no one else's.

· *Hilary Andrewes* ·

SOMEONE TO WATCH OVER ME

Polyhistor sat quietly, her mind still and waiting. Her wings made a gentle "whumpth, whumpth" in the soft breeze; the feathers shimmering where they caught the light. The wings were partly folded and would have made a soft cushion for her back, but Polyhistor sat very straight trying to look not only taller, but older and wiser. Young Ones, and she was a very young One, not even two full eras old, were used to close places, places wrapped in softness in which they felt surrounded and protected. It was almost agony for Polyhistor to sit in this open courtyard with the wide-spaced columns. It was acute distress to gaze up at the pillars and find the eye caught and carried further up, to a place where the pillars almost met . . . but not quite.

She sat where she had been left on the cold bench, staring ahead at the carpet of ferns which swept away into the distance until it shivered into nothingness where it met the purple-blue above it. At times lights hung on the purple-blue and at times they glimmered where the ferns should be, but weren't. Her wings trembled, responding to the racing of her heart, and she dragged her mind back from the edge of fear. Taking deep breaths, she allowed herself to sink into calm, and turned her eyes to the fountain—a very solid, uncompromising fountain, complete with splashing water. She could see where it touched the ferns and when the breeze changed directions, she could feel a slight spray brush her fur. She yearned toward the fountain. Where the basin curved up and away from the ferns there was a small niche, a place she could have cuddled into and felt safe. Instead, she blinked hard and fluttered the feathers of her wings. Then once again Polyhistor sat quietly, her mind still and waiting.

Kate sat quietly, her back propped against the round metal poles that made up the headboard of the bed. She couldn't get comfortable. No matter how she sat, the metal pushed into her back. She'd learned to lean so that her spine was in the space between poles, but she had gotten so thin that her back was permanently bruised from the hard metal. The book lay in her lap where she'd dropped it when her eyes started to go out of focus. She supposed she was reading too much; maybe this afternoon she would play with her paper dolls for awhile.

The older One who had brought Polyhistor to this place appeared in an arch on the far side of the fountain. The fact that she had neither seen nor heard his approach was not betrayed by the slightest flicker in Polyhistor's eyes. The older One was pleased with her control—and somewhat amused—the Propraetor had been right about this One. A smile masked a quick sigh.

"Come, Polyhistor."

So young! She was so young to take this assignment. No one had realized that it was coming this soon, the calculations had been wrong . . . some One would catch it for *that* mistake. There had been no question of Polyhistor's assignment: she would have come of age just in time for that other problem in the charts. Then this sprang up—right out of the Blue (so to speak). Fordel had been assigned to this one. It was in his province and perfect for his skills; it needed just his brand of wisdom and maturity and patience. And then there came that funny quirk and another birth which didn't appear on the Section V charts *at all*, and here they were in the middle of a perfect mess.

It was not easy to be a One, to co-create a life. The rules were unbending, they had to be: co-creation could not be confused with meddling. Ones were all ex-angels, tested and tried and tested again; angels willing to be born into Time out of Eternity. For all creatures existed in Time, and to co-create the life of a creature, to be a guardian, meant binding oneself to Time. And, oh, how painful it was to be cramped, to be pressed and molded where before there had been only freedom! In a sense, Ones provided the woof in the tapestry of existence, just as the planet-bound creatures provided the warp. The metaphor was not perfect, for there were many shuttles carrying many threads, but one thing was true and accepted without question by all Ones: the weaving was done by Another. To meddle was to try to usurp the place of the Weaver and it was the single fault that would remove a One from Time and catapult him firmly back into Eternity. It had only happened once or twice, but the knots in the tapestry were there for all to see—a monument to flawed love.

So here they were, and that cagey old fox Fordel going around as if butter wouldn't melt. You would think that it was common, instead of totally unheard of, for an assignment to be handed off in mid-life. If it weren't for the fact that cross-Section reports were due when the child was only five, she wouldn't have been reviewed until the Ten-Year Breakdown, and by then it would have been too late. As it was, it was unusual for a five-year-old to appear as an individual in the cross-Section reports, but there was Fordel contending that he would have submitted a review with *any* child. Then he had pursed his lips and made one of those irritating, fussy little comments about being thorough.

The older One (whose name was Alaric—a name wished on him by a Senior One left over from the Dark Ages) shook himself and roused from his reverie. Polyhistor was still following, her face intent as she watched the ferns appear before her. He wondered if she realized that he was maintaining them for her, so that she had something solid near her. Older Ones revelled in moving through the absolute openness of the Blue, with only the lights for company.

Alaric returned to his memories of the conversation with Fordel; that strange discussion in which Fordel danced rings around them all, smiling blandly and insisting that he was just fulfilling his assignment. Later, when Fordel had gone, Alaric had spoken to other Ones. They had all been quick to suspect that this was something very big. It seemed like a lot of information was being bandied about, but never—not once!—had he heard the name of the Child. Not once had a reference number been mentioned. They only knew that Fordel had been relieved of the assignment (and seemed *pleased*!) and then, without discussing it with any of the Senior Ones, the Propraetor sent for Polyhistor.

Alaric had volunteered to go to the close places and bring back the young One. Few of the Senior Ones ever returned there once they had lived in the open; most of them felt smothered after the limitless space of the Blue. But Alaric, having some Time on his hands after his last assignment, had taken to visiting the close places to watch the young Ones. He had seen Polyhistor quite by accident one day, curled under a bush in a space so tiny that she had been almost invisible under her folded wings. She was reading and he had been amused by the book she had chosen. He made it a habit to look her up whenever he returned to the close places and, as a result, he had been watching her closely for over a year now. He had suspected for a long time that she was something special . . . now he waited to see just how special.

Kate looked up as her mother breezed into the room, a small dark-haired woman with sparkling brown eyes and snapping energy.

"Hello, kitten-cat. What is it? You look sad."

She laid a cool hand on Kate's head and then plumped up the pillows and smoothed them behind Kate's back where they would feel good for a few minutes until they began to squish down and she felt the poles through them again. "Like the princess and the pea," Kate thought.

"How are the legs, Katy Alex?" Her mother pushed back the

covers and ran her hands firmly over Kate's legs. They looked and felt just like anyone else's legs, a little thin perhaps, but everything about Kate was thin. They just wouldn't hold her up. It seemed to Kate that they were made of rubber. Her mother had tried to trick her into standing up: she would let go of Kate suddenly in the bathroom when Kate was washing her hands, or beside the bed when she stopped to smooth the sheets. It didn't work. Nothing worked.

Kate hadn't heard the doctors telling her parents that it was quite possible Kate would never walk again. They shook their heads and said it was a real shame, such a pretty little girl, but there wasn't much they could do. They didn't say "Polio"; they didn't have to, everyone knew.

Kate wasn't there when her mother told the doctors, "Nonsense!" and her temper flared; "Nonsense!" she had repeated firmly.

Kate was Katherine Alexandra Rhodes; Katy Alex to her father, and sometimes to her mother. She was small and thin and five years old. She had big soft brown eyes ("Like a cow, Katy Alex," her father teased). Her hair was dark brown, with red in it where it caught the sunlight. It fell to her shoulders, and most of the time since she had been confined to bed it was worn in braids to keep it out of her way and out of her eyes. Her skin was very pale. When she grew up and out of the freckles that covered her nose in summer, people would remark on her skin. "So striking—that pale skin and that dark, dark hair. Such a pretty girl!" (*"Pretty,"* her father would think in wry amusement. "It all goes to prove that people don't recognize real *beauty* when they see it . . . .")

At the moment Kate was just a little girl who was sick of being stuck in bed; a little girl who wanted to run and stretch cramped muscles; to be outside for a little while. It wasn't, she thought to herself, as though the bedroom were so awful: it was on the second floor and looked out on treetops and sky. It was always light, even on cloudy days, but it was indoors.

Kate smiled at her mother. "I think I'll take a little nap."

"Okay, kitten, you tuck in and rest. I'll wake you up for a snack later on." Mrs. Rhodes smoothed the covers and kissed Kate's forehead. "Sweet dreams, Kate."

Polyhistor kept walking, the soft pads on her feet sinking pleasantly into the ferns. Occasionally she would lift her eyes and look a bit ahead, past the ferns, past Alaric, to where there was nothing but purple-blue and the lights hung in the vastness. A queasy feeling settled in her stomach and she would look quickly back to the ferns. She became so engrossed that she bumped full-tilt into Alaric who had stopped before a bench on which sat another Senior One.

Alaric's hand reached out to steady her and she looked toward the bench, up, into eyes so grey that they seemed limitless, eyes that kept going in and in, drawing her with them. Alaric's voice called her back from those eyes. "Polyhistor, this is the Propraetor," he said, then added with a touch of Fordel's fussiness, "He wants to talk to you about something very important."

"Of course," Polyhistor smiled. "Of course."

"Alaric, you may go. There is a section meeting of Senior Ones currently in residence. You won't want to miss it."

Alaric, who would have liked nothing better than to miss the meeting if it meant he could remain here, left with carefully disguised impatience. His wings gave him away, ruffling with annoyance as he stalked off. There was no doubt in his mind that Polyhistor was going to be given the assignment (*Fordel's* assignment); it neither shocked him nor surprised him as it did many of the Senior Ones. He was beginning to grasp some of Polyhistor's depth—of course she was raw, but if what he suspected about her was true, her very inexperience was the most precious skill she could bring to this assignment. She would have no preconceived notions, she wouldn't try to fit the Child into a category with tenderness and great humility. There would be no coaxing or prodding from Polyhistor.

Alaric sighed gently. He knew that he was approaching the end of his own term as a One. A few more eras, perhaps, and then he would be thrust back into Eternity, having fulfilled his purpose here. He knew that there were others who would precede him: Fordel, the Propraetor of Section I, a couple of the others at the meeting he would be attending. The Propraetor would decide when the time had come; when his experience and knowledge were keeping him from the sensitivity to nuance that was essential in a One. Occasionally he longed for the rest, more often he felt a hollow ache, knowing that he would miss the intimacy of the work, the beauty of a co-creation which followed the Plan—followed it by love and by choice, for that was the only way the Plan would be fulfilled. When the hollow times came, he would fly out into the Open, far, far from the others, and he would hang suspended, wrapped in his great wings, gazing into the purple-blue, singing with the light, until he was filled again: filled with love and peace and courage.

When Alaric's essence had vanished, the Propraetor motioned Polyhistor to sit and she did, curling up at his feet, snuggled against the bench on which he sat. She did not try to appear older or wiser anymore, for she knew instinctively that she was not on trial with this One. Beside him on the bench, she could see a small, black-bound volume. It measured no more than four and one-half by six inches and was scarcely one-half inch thick. From the top of the book, a single red velvet ribbon, attached to the binding, vanished into the pages. On the cover was a number inscribed in gilt and, below it, a name. Her mind reeled: it was a Reference Book and she knew by the color of the cover that it was from Section VI. Each section had its own color.

In the presence of the Propraetor of Section VI, Elek, one of the most respected and beloved Ones in Time, she slowly pushed herself onto her knees and rested her sensitive finger pads on the bench, gazing at the book. Her mind shied away from the implications of that book on the bench, her wings began to tremble as shudder after shudder passed through her slight form. Her mind fought its way slowly backwards into the lessons she had learned so quickly, so competently, in the close places. She struggled back to the familiar voices of her instructors, the patient voices, the strict voices, the gently firm voices . . . back into the *known*, away from the present moment. The Propraetor sat and watched, seeing the tension and the trembling, the anguish that briefly touched her eyes; and he waited, for the creation of a co-creator is an awe-full moment. Through the stillness of his own essence, he allowed the singing of the lights to reach her; not as melody, but as meaning.

Polyhistor's mind groped through the interweaving voices until, out of the chaos, pattern emerged and she could hear the cool, refreshing tones of Ahimsa, chanting the Sections. After that lesson, she could recall the excitement of her friends. Almost all of them longed for assignments in Section V, which handled most of the VIPs: the statesmen, inventors, artists. There were a few, like Karida, who wanted to work in one of the first four Sections, the group sections, where an assignment might cover two centuries of earth time. But Polyhistor had moved quietly through the excitement, her mind bent on one goal: Section VI, the section which dealt with the "ordinary," "common" people, the individuals who lived close to the fulcrum of the Plan. Oh, yes, Section VI had its share of well-knowns: many of the early Christian saints and martyrs appeared on Section VI charts. Joan of Arc was one of theirs; but, by and large, the assignments were for simple people, caught in the normal pattern of existence, people never singled out for the world's notice.

And she had set herself to learn all that she could about Section VI and its supervisor, Elek. He was a legend in that history, only the second One ever to lead that section. He was known to be wise and fair, with a quick wit and a sure hand. Well, she reflected, he would have to be with some of the Senior Ones who served under him, Ones with strong personalities who could do their best work only with minimal supervision.

Polyhistor looked up, and was once again drawn into those

eyes. They seemed not to reflect at all, as if they had no surface. They were inviting eyes, honest and vulnerable. In them she saw a strong but flexible will, an inherent kindness, the pain of eras of suffering overlaid with a sense of humor polished and honed by centuries of hard work and responsibility. Deep within Polyhistor a knot loosened, she smiled and watched an answering smile bubble up from the depths of Elek's spirit. The warm voice spoke.

"It is Time, Polyhistor?"

"The Time is Now and I am Here," her voice stumbled slightly over the unfamiliar ritual. "The light has called, and in its singing I heard my name."

"The shuttle has left the hand of the Weaver. Will you watch its pattern?"

"I will," she replied, finishing the chant.

"Dear Oneling, this will not be easy for you. You will have to leave the close places and live here in the Open. You have learned all you need, but you will not know it yet." Elek smiled at the trust in Polyhistor's eyes. "You will be torn and troubled and afraid that you will do harm. It is all right to fear, Polyhistor, we have all known fear, it is a creature of Time; but you more than most will know it because you have had no practice with the old Reference Books. You do not really understand that mistakes are part of co-creation, and until you know that, you will always fear. There is no One else I wished to trust with this assignment. I am glad you heard your name."

Polyhistor bowed her head and rested it against the coolness of the bench. She did not reach yet for the book, although she knew now that it was hers. She had known from the moment when, through the voices in her head, the call had come. She had known in that instant the meaning of the lights which hung in the purple-blue, she had heard their names and she had felt her own name, woven with them. If she had had any doubts, she was bound by the Rule to leave the chant unfinished, but the discordance would have grated harshly on her ears, and so she had resolved the chord and finished the ritual, which bound her to this assignment for whatever years it might take.

She did not know Fordel, although in the days ahead she would become familiar with his beautiful copperplate hand which filled the first few pages of the book on the bench. She did not know that in giving up this assignment, he had cast himself into voluntary exile until it was completed—for he could be given no other assignment while he was bound to this. She did not yet understand a love which could offer such a sacrifice because she could not remember Eternity and the face of the Weaver. In the eons ahead, it would become clearer and clearer until it called her back from Time into Eternity. Now it was only a barely tangible presence heard in the singing of the light.

Elek waited and watched, marveling again that it was the property of Propraetors to wait and watch. His uncanny sensitivity to the Ones he supervised let him guess what lay behind Polyhistor's stillness. In these moments she was carefully wrapping up the thoughts and sensations of her short time in the close places, putting them away—storing them against the millennia of life in the Open. She was saying a silent goodbye to friends she might not see again for centuries, to the freedom and warmth of her youth. Elek watched what was now so calm that it could no longer be called a struggle—and his spirit leapt out to meet the serenity of this young One. He ached to gather her to him, to smooth the small training wings she had not yet outgrown. Yet she had completed the chant, she was now a Senior One, however young, however small, however marked.

While he watched, she lifted her head and focussed on the Reference Book. One hand went out to touch the cover and draw it toward her across the cool bench. She lifted it very gently and held it in both hands. On the cover were two lines. The first was a reference number: CH19   51:   28*09   sec6. Below it, inscribed in beautiful letters, was a name: Katherine Alexandra Rhodes.

Mary McDermott Shideler

We human beings are guilty far too often of wanting everything to be even. We want, as much as possible, to do something for someone and to get back something from that same person. How much healthier it is for our psyches that life doesn't seem to work in such closed systems; how fortunate that we often receive blessings or love in such a way that we cannot "pay back," but must rather "pass on," the gift. In this way the system stays open and the movement of love is outward, away from the self.

In the course of the letters we have exchanged while this anthology was taking shape, Mary and I have discussed in some depth the concept of the open system. In this story it exists in one of its most basic and beautiful forms; Mary attributes the idea as she uses it here to Charles Williams.

In thinking about "Mother and the Flying Saucer" and in writing this introduction, I have come to the conclusion that the open system is a duty according to the standards of the Heinlein definition quoted in the introduction to this book. It is something I owe myself as a direct result of a commitment I have accepted voluntarily as a member of the human race. I have a responsibility to keep the direction of love spiraling outward. The responsibility becomes mine because I accept it, and accepting it brings with it joy and growth and the space in which to expand. In choosing to reach outward, we choose a larger forum, a greater openness. We may not feel as protected as we would in a closed room, but we have space to run and dance, to explore not only our world, but a freer self.

MOTHER AND
THE FLYING SAUCER

Mother was planting tulips around the farmhouse when she saw it: a silvery, lentil-shaped object an inch or an inch and a quarter across. It lay close to the sack of bulbs in the thin sunshine. Without really thinking, she reached out her hand to pick it up. It had a smooth, cool texture to her fingers, something like metal, something like water, something like the cheek of a child when it comes in from playing in the snow. But she distinctly had not lifted it. It had come in her hand of its own accord, moving and sustaining itself.

Like a good many people who are in or above their seventies, Mother had far more courage and curiosity than fear when faced with something strange. Naturally she was startled, but she was not afraid. So she looked at it. After a moment, she tried turning it over. Instead, it turned itself over, as if it were responding instantaneously to her thought. It looked, and felt, just the same on the other side.

Sometime along in these first seconds, she realized that it was not heavy, as she had expected it to be when she reached for it. In fact, it had no weight at all. Before that idea had been formulated clearly, the thing began to press down on her hand, slowly increasing its downward push, then equally slowly releas-

33

ing its pressure until again it lay upon her hand without resting there.

By now, Mother was genuinely astonished, although still not frightened. Her habit of examining things before she reacted to them stood her in good stead. She tried tossing it gently, as one tosses a coin into the air. It rose perhaps six inches, twirled around a couple of times in a way she had not planned, and returned to the palm of her hand.

All this time, Mother had been squatting on her heels, but her knees were getting stiff, so she sat back with her legs out, to consider the situation and quiet her mind. She had lived alone on the farm for the many years since my father had died and I had taken a teaching post in the East, and the solitude had deepened her essentially contemplative spirit. Therefore she knew her way from excitement into stillness, from accident to substance. To use her own phrase for it, she paused and considered.

In the midst of her consideration, the thing rose from her hand of its own accord. It hung motionless in the air in front of her until she was wholly intent upon it, and then it began to dance. Twisting, spiraling, first gravely and then swiftly, it dove and soared and turned. And through the dance came a sound, a lucid monotone like a vertical rod, around which it whirled.

Mother could never explain how she knew that the dance was a salutation. She used to compare it with the way that one recognizes a color as gloomy or a line as flowing. But she did know and she was entranced, not only with the princely grace of its actions, but with its intentions—with the fact that so clearly it had an intention. It was a being, not a thing, and she laughed aloud.

It was only later, when she described the event to me, that she realized how fearless she had been, and comprehended the reason. Partly, of course, it resulted from her personal courage. But in part it was because the thing's own direct friendliness had acted to forestall any terror. It could not prevent surprise, but it could endow surprise with delight. Mother felt quite like a small girl who has unexpectedly found herself at a circus.

When the thing had again settled just off the ground in front of her, trembling a little for all the world as if it were panting for breath and trying not to giggle, Mother wondered what she should do next. Common hospitality suggested that she invite it into the house, perhaps for a cup of tea, as she would any other guest. On the other hand, she had no idea what it ate, if anything, or even how, since it seemed to have no orifice for a mouth. But she could think of nothing to do except offer it what she had. With an acute sense of her absurdity, she rose, brushed the leaves and grass from her slacks, and with trowel in one hand, the sack of bulbs in the other, she looked hopefully at the thing. No etiquette book prescribes how to behave in these circumstances, but in all good-fellowship, feeling frustrated and exceedingly foolish and oddly happy, she managed the words, "Won't you come in and have some tea?"

It rose, bobbed slightly as if bowing, and accompanied her in.

She made two cups of tea, and finally drank both of them. By then she had some idea of what or who her guest was, and where it had come from, but not why. It communicated by some form of telepathy which produced pictures and meaning at once. It answered questions freely, but either it had no ability to force its ideas upon her, or else it was too courteous to try, because it asked permission, so to speak, before affecting her thoughts. Indeed, after the first minutes when it was introducing itself, never at any time during the period of their companionship did it give any indication whatsoever of reading her mind except as she addressed herself to it. She could be over in the north eighty, wish for its company, and almost immediately it would be at her side, but if she merely thought about it instead of to it, it seemed to have no awareness of what was going on in her mind.

She did not try to figure out which planet it had come from, although she knew from what it "told" her that its home was one of those in our solar system, and existing in our time-space configuration. It did not have a name. It was identified among the rest of its kind (and there were many thousands of others) by its single and unique musical tone. When two of the things met in their own place, each uttered its distinctive tone, and they danced together for a moment before they went their ways. They did not eat or drink or breathe; they did not grow or give birth or die. Structurally they were homogeneous, differing slightly from each other in diameter (roughly one to four inches), depth (about three-eighths to one and a half inches), and the exact tint of their silvery color. They had no verbal language, communicating by the three methods to which Mother had already been introduced: by the sound peculiar to each, by patterns of movement, and by telepathic transmission of images, this last being immensely facilitated by the universal perfection of their memories. It cannot properly be said that they "saw" and "heard" with parts of their "bodies," because their bodies were not differentiated into parts, or their perceptions into types of sensation. The integral thing was a single instrument of awareness, of motion, and of identity.

All this Mother discovered on this first afternoon of their acquaintance. It was late when she noticed her hunger, and bethought herself both of supper and of the news broadcast that was as much a part of her daily routine as her meals. Half apologetically, she conferred with her guest, who swooped over to the television set and without apparent effort, nudged the control and turned it on. While an ancient movie ground to its inadequate close, Mother pulled a prepared dinner from the freezer and put it into the oven.

I also saw and heard that newscast, and remember it clearly, even to such surrounding details as the stack of ungraded test papers on top of the TV set and the sound of the autumn rain on the street outside my apartment, a thousand miles from where Mother was having strange company at dinner. The commentator's personal excitement was not quite masked under the rather forced humor with which he read the official Defense Department bulletin to the effect that an odd phenomenon had been reported a few hours earlier. Small bits of what appeared to be metal had turned up at various places in the United States and elsewhere. So far as was known, they had been found all over the world at

approximately the same time: between three and four in the afternoon, Central Standard Time. The things obviously were
harmless, added the commentator a little grimly, and probably
had been scattered by the dissolution in mid-air of one of the
artificial satellites, although none of these had yet been reported
missing. It was quite possible that a prankster had sown them from
a plane, for some unknown reason. The Defense Department had
put scientists to work investigating these things, and anyone who
found such an object (a hastily constructed model was shown)
was bidden to call his local police department, which would check
the evidence and forward the thing to the appropriate authorities.
There followed the weather report and other news of the day,
which for once Mother completely ignored.

Her first impulse was to notify the police, not an easy business
on an eight-party rural line at that hour of the evening, but she
felt that cooperation was one of the courtesies owed by the citizen
to his government and therefore worth the effort. Almost at once,
however, she hesitated, then turned to her guest. To explain? To
ask its pleasure? To . . . ? Motives are chancy things. She sat
back in her chair and tucked one leg firmly beneath her. "There's
no hurry about this, little friend. We'll wait and see."

The following morning, news reports were reassuring as to inci-
dent, but gave the impression of terror controlled with difficulty.
The newspaper was hysterically calm. Headlines referred to "Flying
Saucers," and in spite of official derogation of the name, the title
stuck. The things were reported as having landed at one of the
atomic research laboratories in England, at the Mount Wilson
observatory (where it had been identified as having come from
Uranus), at a coal mine in West Virginia where the miners
promptly went out on strike, at a filling-station in Deckers,
Colorado, and a number of other places. The carilloneur at a
famous French cathedral had disappeared, together with a Saucer
that had been present—according to four impeccable witnesses—
at a vesper service. Business was continuing as usual, except for

the number of traffic snarls caused by the absence of police officers who had been transferred to the so-called Saucer Squads.

Within a few days, the furor quieted down somewhat. Three hundred and seventy-eight reports of sightings had been authenticated. The United Nations had appointed a committee. The Joint Chiefs of Staff had met and recessed. The British Cabinet had issued a White Paper. *Pravda* and the Vatican united in urging caution. The Executive Committee of the World Council of Churches had made a statement. So had the Dalai Lama, the Dictator of Merovingia, the Peruvian Minister of External Relationships, and the Secretary of the Los Angeles Chamber of Commerce. All of them reiterated, so clearly and so often, that the Flying Saucers were completely innocuous, that nearly everybody believed the invaders to be capable of both the wish and the ability to destroy all mankind, and (or) were planning to govern the entire world and enslave its inhabitants, and (or) were performing miscellaneously horrible feats that were never defined at all.

The Great Saucer Panic, however, is not a part of Mother's story, except as she deplored it, and as her friendship with her particular Flying Saucer was concealed, first by her ordinary reticence, and then by her determination not to betray her friend. Even I knew nothing about it until my annual trip to spend Christmas with Mother at the farm.

Everyone knew, by Christmastime, that the Saucers were unaffected by even the extremes of temperature, or by pressures measured in megatons, or by nuclear fission, or by anything else known to man. One of them had been placed so as to receive the full impact of an H-bomb test, and a couple of minutes after the blast, while one of the scientists was wishing he could test the Saucer then and there, it appeared suddenly then and there at the apparatus which he wished to use. After exhaustive examination, it was discovered to be no more radioactive than when it had first appeared two months previously—which was somewhat less than matter in this world usually is. Nor had it altered in any other respect that could be determined. Further, none of the other investigations by physical scientists, biologists, social scientists, psychologists, linguists, statisticians, or students of ESP produced any other or better information.

On Christmas Eve, Mother finally risked taking her friend away from the farm. She invited it to go with us to the midnight service at St. Thomas's. We had talked about her carrying it in her purse, or up the full sleeve of the dress she intended to wear, but when the time came and she raised with it the question of its hiding-place, it soared over to her and slipped into the hollow above her left collarbone, where it lay cool against her skin, secure from sight beneath her dress, and out of her way when she moved. It was not held there by her clothing, but by its own action. It did not fall simply because it never fell anyway: it had no weight of its own, only pressure which it varied at its own will.

Both Mother and I were acutely aware of its presence with us, and of the dangers of discovery. All Flying Saucers were being confiscated even at that time, and an individual who had not been cleared to study them was liable to severe penalties for having one in his possession. Mother had asked my advice about this, early during my visit, but I could see no reason for her to relinquish her friend, since it was a friend. Even the top authorities agreed publicly that they had plenty of specimens to work on, and that the only reason for sequestering them was the general fear that sometime they might possibly prove dangerous to someone. Neither then nor later was there any evidence to support this fear, except for the single instance of the disappearing Parisian carilloneur who (as everybody admitted) might have departed his post or this life for any of several good reasons totally unconnected with the Saucers.

We were silent on our way into town, not with apprehension, but from the lateness of the hour and in preparation for the service. So we moved easily from the atmosphere of the farm house and the drive, to the festive mood of the church. For the prelude, the organist gave us Bach. The choir and the priest came in with, "O Come, All Ye Faithful." We had reached "Sing, choirs of angels" when I realized that while the rest of the congregation seemed completely normal, Mother had stopped singing. Her face was deathly white and intensely alive. My first thought was for her; my second, instantly, for—and to—the Saucer. And then I also saw and heard. Outwardly we followed the service, kneeling and sitting and standing, speaking the holy words, but meanwhile. . . .

It was deep night in the forest. The light of the two pale moons then above the horizon did not penetrate it. Not that it was a forest in our sense: Uranus has no woods like ours, but this was the Uranian counterpart. Nor was I seeing in our sense: that absolute sable allowed no use of earthly eyes. But I did know that beyond my visual perception were the two moons; I perceived as if visually the forest; and I heard as if with ears the high, single, sustained note, brilliant but not piercing, mellow but without overtones. A second note joined it, in a harmony rounding out the beauty of the first. There was a long interval while they reverberated together in an almost unendurable perfection of sound. A third note entered, swiftly followed by two more. To harmony was added another quality which is not like anything in our world except rhythm, but this was not rhythm. It was a pulsing, syncopated, sprung irregularity, a release and a creation of life, adoration and impossible joy, aspiration and longing, illimitable despair and a plea.

Into the incredible chord came a new note. The pattern altered, some voices silencing themselves, others moving in to form a new diagram of beauty. The changes came more swiftly, each resolution making place for another, every peak of ecstasy bringing forth a more intense, more complex culmination, all informed with the same passion of worship and despair.

At last, mercifully, it withdrew from me. I could not have endured that exaltation much longer, and lived.

I have heard it once since that holy night. I expect to hear it only once more—when I die.

When we reached home after the service, Mother and I had a glass of sherry while we learned the rest of the story from the Saucer. What we had heard—seen—sensed—was the Uranian's worship of God, but it was also the creation of a new Uranian. It was the way by which the Saucers formed new beings of their kind.

I can write of what it told us only as if it were using words.

"We differ from humanity of Earth in being entirely integrated, having one substance, one intention, one sound. It is our delight to be so complete in ourselves, but also our abiding and terrible grief. You cannot know, you who change in body and mood and idea and purpose, you who can utter so many words, how it is to be not simply single-minded, but utterly single in strength and awareness. We do not even sleep. We can vary our movements. We can perceive differences. But we are always identical. You people achieve singleness as you unite with others; we find with others our only experience of difference—of variation as something felt, not merely observed. And only in the adoration and creation that you have seen do we come close to the complexity that we seek. You cannot know how we desire to be divided, because you already have that gift of separation. All men have it. We have come, some of us, to try to learn it from you."

I was stupid. "What gift?" I asked, and it replied, "Death."

It had lived long enough among us to comprehend that division in itself—death or double-mindedness or difference of sex and intellect and attitude and value—is scarcely an unmixed blessing. But also, as Mother was well aware, the fact of being complex has its points, and unmitigated integration, even in combination with natural immortality, may be as appalling as conflict joined with foreordained mortality. So she immediately offered to do whatever she could to help it in its search, the more eargerly because it explained that the failure of the scientists to destroy its companions had disappointed all the Saucers severely. They had been particularly hopeful of the H-bomb experiment, and they all— those still on Uranus and those on our earth—had joined in a special convocation of worship with and for the one who had been chosen to undergo the test.

The general situation remained essentially unchanged for almost two years. After the Christmas Eve service at St. Thomas's, Mother usually took her Saucer along when she went into town for any reason, social or business, church or shopping. A few of her close friends commented that she looked more vigorous than usual, but none of them knew about her companion, or guessed that her new vitality sprang from the happiness of their relationship. I gathered from her letters that she was entertaining a little more than she had during the previous ten years or so, but she did not explain whether this was because she was invited out more frequently, or because she was actually stronger. She referred to the Saucer only indirectly in her letters, using "we" without specifying who or what else had been involved, although as the public strain relaxed, the regulations against private or individual commerce with the Saucers had been withdrawn. In fact, quite a few people kept them around as curiosities or pets. They were wonderful for entertaining small children, playing with them almost as a puppy does, or letting themselves be used as balls, and never permitting the youngsters to get into mischief.

It was in September, nearly two years after the first appearance of the Flying Saucers, that Mother had her automobile accident, when she was on her way to visit me for a week before my classes started. The car ahead of her had slowed for a left turn. The car behind her was going too fast to stop. She was the only person in the three cars who survived, and she was dreadfully injured. She was seventy-six, and frail. I reached the hospital only an hour or two before she finally regained consciousness after the long, long surgery putting her back together.

She awoke for a moment the next morning, and recognized me. She could not speak, but after her eyes had welcomed me, they questioned, and it dawned on me that she was asking about her Saucer. It was not there and could not be found. Apparently it had disappeared without trace or sign. The next day, when she had another lucid interval, I told her that it was gone. Momentarily she seemed puzzled, then there spread over her face a look of the most intense satisfaction that I have ever seen. No—not satisfaction. Triumph.

Her response left me utterly bewildered. Her beloved friend, her intimate companion, was gone as if it had died, and yet she looked triumphant. The phrase "as if it had died" was no more than a verbal habit, but it leaped back at me. The Saucer had died. I took another step. It had died for her.

I got as far as that in my thinking, and there my muddled brain stopped. The next stage of understanding came much later, when Mother was well enough to discuss the affair and to be impatient with my dullness. The Saucer had not merely died for her, it had died instead of her. Its love had enabled it to take into itself that death that reached for her, and so it was that she lived. It had died her death.

Four years later, at the time of my heart attack, Mother died my death for me. Now it is my turn. One of these days, I shall die someone else's death.

Strange, what a difference it makes, confronting another's death in me instead of my own. I wonder whose death it will be.

Madeleine L'Engle

I discovered Madeleine L'Engle's books during my adolescence when their wisdom and love brought me through some of the universal, but nonetheless painful, experiences which mark those years. I was naturally thrilled when she agreed to write a story for this book. My immediate reaction when I got to the last page was the same as Jonathan's: "But Master—." A friend once remarked that one of the things he found most amusing about Christians was that while they professed a firm belief in God, they always seemed to be applying for his job. How true. I had already decided what the miracle in the title was going to be and, as so often happens, had decided that nothing else was appropriate.

It is often difficult to remember that great flaws or weaknesses tend to conceal within themselves great strengths and gifts. A friend, a brilliant and talented young woman with multiple sclerosis, recently said, "It is no garden of roses, but I have been given a great gift along with the problems: I have more time for people; I have more time for *now*. No: I will never have the career I planned, but I have been able to put that behind me. And the lack of anguish is the *real* miracle; I have bad days when I want to scream, "Why ME!?", but they are fewer than I have any right to expect."

Annie Dillard, in her glorious book *Pilgrim at Tinker Creek*, remarked, "The world is fairly studded with pennies cast broadside from a generous hand." Every one of those pennies is a gift, yet how often we walk away from those gifts quite without concern—and then complain because life holds no wonder and no miracle. "The One Hundred and First Miracle" is for all of us who have ever—even once—complained about the size of the gift.

44

· Madeleine L'Engle ·

THE ONE HUNDRED AND FIRST MIRACLE

By the time Miriam was fifteen she was a constant embarrassment to her family, and her mother told her to her face that she was a disgrace.

"And I don't have to be told what the neighbours think," her mother continued. "I don't know what I did to deserve a daughter like you."

"Leave her alone," Daniel, the brother who sometimes took her part, spoke up. "It isn't her fault."

"Isn't it? Whose is it then? Tell me that."

Miriam let the talk move like a hot desert wind over her head. She had long since accepted the fact that her parents and most of her brothers and sisters and certainly all of the neighbours considered the fact that she had gone blind when she was a little girl to be the result of sin rather than disease. She did not know what she had done, but evidently it was something very bad, if this was the punishment, and she moved always under a heavy weight of guilt for an unknown crime. And daily she added to the guilt. She did not sit in a corner and keep out of everybody's way as a blind girl ought to do. She walked the streets of the town and the highways and the byways of the country and what's more, she walked with a dog. There had been a bitter family clash over the dog.

"Dogs are filthy animals," her mother said. "Nobody has dogs."

The inflamed remains of Miriam's eyes seemed to stare defiantly at her mother. "I have a dog," she said.

"You're not to bring the dirty creature into the house."

"He doesn't want to come into the house." This, Miriam knew, was not true, and she was adding to her sins with a deliberate lie. The dog, whom she had named Samson, wanted to be anywhere that Miriam was, and this in itself was unusual, for the dogs in the village were not friendly, were, instead, lean and hungry beasts who ran through the streets, jaws slavering. According to Miriam's mother, Samson was hideous, mud coloured, with ferocious yellow teeth. Miriam remembered colours, and as far as she was concerned, Samson was a deep purply grey, and his mouth infinitely gentle as he held her hand between his jaws in order to lead her around rocks or rough places where she might stumble. Miriam could not have gone on her long walks without Samson. She would not have had her friends. The friends she had to keep secret from her parents, whom she told that she went to the end of the village where there was a great pile of rocks, and there she sat and thought. This was at least partly true. She did. But she went other places, too, places which would be forbidden her if ever her family discovered them.

This, she knew, was not likely. She was allowed to keep Samson and to leave the house in the morning and not come back until evening because it kept her out of sight and out of mind. No one knew where she went, and as long as the neighbours had lost their curiosity, her mother did not care. Miriam would take some bread and cheese and a small skin of wine and set off in the morning, and people had become so accustomed to seeing her leaving the village with Samson that it had long since ceased to be a topic of discussion. Miriam was a disgrace, of course, and the family to be pitied because of her, but it was a dull day when there wasn't some spicier gossip than where Miriam and the dog went and what they did.

Near the gates was the house which belonged to Esther, the harlot. Esther was one of Miriam's friends. They had known each other since Miriam was ten, and had found Samson—or had Samson found Miriam—and she had been able to move away from the house on her own. In the early days of the walks, even with her hand on Samson's head, or in his mouth, she was apt to stumble and fall. As long as she didn't skin her knees too badly she didn't care; all she knew was that she needed to get out of the house, that when she was at home she could not breathe; it was almost as though there were a physical constriction about her chest, so that she could not grow up, she could not be Miriam, whoever Miriam was, unless she got away.

She fell, one day, just as Esther the harlot, yawning and sleepy, was coming out of her house. This time Miriam did skin her knees badly. She had trained herself never to cry out when she bumped herself or fell, so she was picking herself up in angry silence, holding her lips tightly together, when she felt arms around her. She jerked away.

"Why, you poor little thing," a wine-dark voice said. "Who hits you? I'm not going to hurt you."

"I'm all right," Miriam said sharply.

"You're not all right at all. Your knees are covered with blood and you've spilt your wine skin and I don't know which has made the worse mess, the blood or the wine."

"My mother will be furious—" Miriam started.

"Come on," the voice said. "The dog can come too, if you like. I'd better clean you up. What are you doing wandering about on your own?"

"I'm being *me!*" Miriam shouted, and to her intense surprise and dismay she burst into tears.

"I'm Esther," the smoky voice continued calmly. "That's who I am. Who are you?"

"I'm Miriam." The words came out, muffled, through sobs. After a while she realized that she was sitting down, that Esther was gently washing her knees, and then her face. Then she felt a comb being worked through the mats of her hair.

"Doesn't your mother ever comb your hair?"

"Sometimes. But she likes it to hide my eyes."

A cool hand gently pushed her hair back. "You poor little thing, you."

"I am not—" Miriam started angrily, but the woman laughed, a small bubbling of merriment.

"Don't be so ferocious. I admit your mother has a point. Otherwise you might turn out to be quite beautiful."

"It's sinful to lie," Miriam said.

"People like me can't be bothered with lying." The comb continued to pull softly at the tangled hair.

"I get told often enough how ugly I am," Miriam said. "Sometimes I'm almost glad I can't see myself if I'm that ugly."

Hands held her cheeks, tilted her head back. Esther spoke dispassionately. "Your hair is filthy. I'll have to see about washing it. You have beautiful skin, and it's going to be more beautiful as you grow older. Your bone structure couldn't be better. Your eyes, I grant you, are red and matted and quite nasty to look at. I'll get you a bit of pretty cloth to tie about them."

"Why are you being nice to me?" Miriam asked. "I don't have anything to give you, and my parents don't either."

"You don't have to give me anything. I don't like to see a child who gets beaten and kicked. Who hits you?"

Miriam shrugged. "Everyone except Daniel sometimes. He's one of my brothers. The others say he's soft."

"You're too thin," Esther said. "Don't they feed you? Or can't they?"

"Oh, yes, we eat very well. It's just that I'd rather take my food and keep out of everybody's way. I don't spill as much when I'm by myself."

"What are we going to do about your dress?" Esther asked. "It's all bloody and covered with wine. I'd better wash it. It will dry in an hour in the sun. I'll put it up on the roof."

Miriam was given a soft robe of a material she had never felt before, tender and luxurious. Her fingers moved appreciatively over the stuff.

"It's silk," Esther told her. "It was given me by a traveller from

Arabia. By the way, little Miriam, I wouldn't say anything about
me when you get home if I were you."

"I wouldn't."

"My name is not well, perhaps they might not approve of your
associating with me."

"All they care about is not having me underfoot and not having
the neighbours talk about me. I'm the family disgrace."

Again came Esther's bubbling laugh. "That makes two of us,
little one."

"And Samson makes three." Miriam's hand reached out and
fondled the dog's ear.

"I'm surprised," Esther said in her cool, dark voice, "that the
animal lets them hit you."

"He wouldn't if he were allowed in the house, and then it
would be awful because they really wouldn't let me keep him if
he tried to interfere."

"I can see that you're a great trial to them. You don't have a
properly humble attitude and you take up with a dirty dog—he
needs a bath, too—and now me."

Oh, yes, Miriam did indeed take up with Esther the harlot.
Knowing Esther was the most illuminating thing that had ever
happened to her. Esther gave her beautiful things to feel, a lion
carved out of jade, cool in the palm of the hand; necklaces of
strange-shaped beads; earrings and bracelets of precious stones
and metals; various textures of foreign stuffs, all brought her by
travellers from distant lands. She gave Miriam a heavy comb of
tortoise-shell, and bits of silk to tie about her eyes; these blind-
folds she washed when they got soiled; and she taught Miriam to
keep her body clean and fragrant.

"You really are learning," she said approvingly one day. "Your
hair is glossy and pleasant to touch and it no longer smells like a
stable. When you're a little older maybe I'll give you some perfumed oils, but not yet. What does your family say?"

Miriam held her hands out towards Esther and smiled. "Not
much. I take the ribbon off my eyes before I go back in to the

village, and I mess up my hair, otherwise they'd get curious and try to stop me from coming here. And then I'd die. When I'm with you I don't have that awful weight on my shoulders."

"What weight, child?"

"Oh, of being bad."

"What makes you think you're bad?"

Miriam took her hands out of Esther's and raised them to her eyes. "My mother says it's a punishment for my sins, and she and all the family are made to suffer because of me."

Esther rose and walked around the room. "I think I am too angry to speak. What can I say, child? I'll tell you one thing. I know a lot about sin. And I know a lot about the world. In my opinion it's the good people who get horrible eye diseases and things even worse—and there are a great many things that are a great deal worse. And it's the sinners who flourish and get the rewards. Sins and punishments don't go together. So forget about it."

Miriam heard her move with the gentle swish of her silken garments back to her soft couch and sit down. Miriam was seated on a cushion beside the couch, and she leaned back against Esther's knees. "Why do you bother with me?"

Esther gave the amused gurgle which Miriam loved. "Someone has to. Now, child, run along. I have a traveller coming from Tarshish."

It was on one of the days when Esther told her to "run along" that Miriam met Jonathan.

An hour's walk beyond Esther the harlot's house was a hillside leading in to some caves. On the hillside and in the caves were rock-hewn tombs and it was here among the dead that the living dead, the lepers, lived. On the first day on which Esther approached the caves she stopped, hand on Samson's head, sniffing; there was a terrible odour, thick and sweetish. She felt people close around her, and then they were yelling at her, telling her to go away. She was surrounded by anger and rage, and in her fear she lost all sense of direction and blundered closer to the caves.

"Leave her alone," a voice said. "She's blind and she's still a child. I'll take care of it." It was an old voice, and it carried authority. Miriam felt a withdrawing of the bodies about her.

The voice said, "If you will move a few feet to your right and hold out your hand, you will feel a rock. Sit on it."

Miriam obeyed. Samson pressed close against her and she realized that he was growling deep in his throat.

"Hold your dog."

Miriam put a restraining hand against Samson.

"What are you doing here?"

"I was just walking."

"Why?"

"I couldn't stay with Esther, and I didn't want to go home."

"Do you know where you are?"

Miriam held up her face. "How would I know?"

"Or who we are?"

Now a second voice spoke, a young voice. "Let me talk to her, Uncle."

"Be quiet, Jonathan."

"Uncle, don't tell her—"

"She has a right to know. We are lepers, child. We are the unclean."

Miriam sat still upon the rock and said nothing.

"Listen," the young voice, Jonathan's voice said, "if you want to talk, we won't touch you. You can sit on the rock, and we can talk, and you'll be all right."

"Why do you want to talk to me?" she asked.

"Because you're beautiful."

She held out both hands in an odd, pushing gesture, as though to thrust aside his words. Then she turned her palms inward as though pulling them back. Esther had almost made her believe that she was pleasing to look upon, despite the continued disparagement she got at home.

"Be honest, Jonathan," the old voice said.

"I am, Uncle! I speak the truth! She is beautiful."

"Yes. But beauty is not all you want from her."

"He means food," Jonathan explained. "We don't have enough to eat. People bring us food at night and put it here near the rock you're sitting on, but it is not enough. Uncle tries to see that it is divided fairly, but as usual the strong get more and the weak get less. That is the way of the world."

"I'll give you half my bread and cheese," Miriam said. "And perhaps Esther will give me something for you. But I can't bring it at night or my family'd find out."

"And we couldn't look at you at night," the young voice said. "I am Jonathan. What is your name?"

"I am Miriam." So their friendship began.

Just as Esther gave Miriam things to feel, educating her sense of touch, so Jonathan gave Miriam things to see through his vivid power of description. Miriam half guessed that Jonathan did not report to her things as they were, but things as he thought they ought to be. For instance, he described himself as being tall and olive-skinned, with sea-grey eyes; he had a strong, lean body with beautifully proportioned limbs. The other lepers he described in the same manner. "Small Anna has the most extraordinary golden curls that catch the fire of the sun. And her eyes are the blue of the sky. Her fingers are long and white and tender."

"Anna's fingers—" someone started. Miriam heard Jonathan swing around, and the demurring voice ceased.

Once Uncle said, in a low voice, but Miriam's quick ears heard, "Jonathan, you should not lie to Miriam."

"I do not lie," Jonathan replied. "This is what we are really like. This is the real truth."

When Miriam asked Esther for food for the lepers, Esther was horrified. "You are not to go near them! I forbid you, absolutely forbid you to go to the Hill of the Caves again."

"They don't touch me," Miriam said. "I sit on the rock and they gather round and we talk. But they never touch me."

"Don't be a fool," Esther said. "Do you want to get leprosy on top of everything?"

"I will not get leprosy."

"Sometimes I think you are more a mule than a girl. Do you

know what lepers look like?"

"Yes. Jonathan tells me."

"Who is Jonathan?"

"One of them."

"And does he tell you that their fingers fall off, and their noses? That their skin hangs in repulsive sores from their bones? Or if he doesn't, can't you smell?"

"I smell better than you do."

("Samuel has dark curls and rosy cheeks," Jonathan said. "He's as strong as a leopard, and as graceful." And, "Ruth is new among us. She is beautiful, as beautiful as you are, but she is sad. You must help her to be merry.")

"I forbid you to go near them. Of course I won't give you any food for them."

"If I just leave food by the rock, the way it's done at night?"

"If others leave food, why should you?"

"Because there isn't enough. Some of them die of hunger."

"All right," Esther said. "But you are just to leave the food. What would happen to me if you got leprosy and brought it back to me?"

At first Miriam lied by omission. Then the weight on her shoulders began to oppress her even more than usual. She was happy with the lepers, not only with Jonathan, but with all of them who loved to hear her tell stories. She told them all the stories which she had heard in the village, and, far better than these, all the stories which Esther had heard from her travellers from foreign lands. Esther told the stories in her usual cool, factual manner, and then Miriam took them and wove them with the brightly coloured threads of her imagination. She described strange garments and houses, drawing on her small store of memory of colour and shape. She learned that by spinning a story out, by pausing at the crucial moment, she could have the lepers gasping and hanging on her words. And she told them funny stories and the stinking air was lightened with laughter.

And she brought them food from Esther, and, with Jonathan and Uncle beside her and Samson ready to growl, it was divided fairly.

Only dimly did she realize that the most important gift she brought them was her blindness, for thus she saw them as Jonathan described them to her, for thus she saw them as they knew themselves to be.

But Esther's words echoed in her head and the weight of them pressed down on her. "What would happen to me if you got leprosy and brought it back to me?"

For a week she hurried past Esther's house. She had told her brother Daniel that she was hungry, and indeed she looked thinner than usual, for she gave away half of her bread and cheese, so he talked their mother into giving her more.

"I give her plenty," their mother said. "I suppose she's got some wasting disease now on top of everything else. She is a wicked, wicked girl and I'm sure I've done nothing to deserve such a burden." But she gave Miriam a double portion to keep her out of sight.

After a week Esther was still waiting for Miriam. "All right, now. What is this?"

"I can't come to see you any more."

"Why not?"

"Because I'm seeing the lepers."

Esther's voice was cold. "You prefer the lepers to me?"

"I love you!" Miriam cried, and a sob rose in her throat so that her words came out in a strange and muffled manner.

"Then why do you want to hurt me?"

"I don't! Oh, Esther, you know I don't! That's why I haven't come. So that I couldn't possibly hurt you!"

Esther sighed, and Miriam shivered with relief as the older woman's hand passed tenderly over her hair. "You are the child I can never have," Esther said. "Why must you go to the lepers?"

Miriam's voice was low. "They need me."

Esther sighed again. "Come in. Your dress needs tending again. And I'll get you some food."

"But—"

"I have never believed in acting out of fear," Esther said. "What we fear comes and hangs itself about our necks. I know you well enough to know that if I forbid you to go to the lepers you will go anyhow. You are a wicked, disobedient girl and I understand perfectly why your mother beats you. You promise me that you do not let them touch you? Ever?"

"I would let them," Miriam said. "But they wouldn't."

"Come in," Esther said again, taking Miriam's hand. "But leave the dog outside this time. There's no point in taking unnecessary risks."

So Esther continued to feed the lepers with her food, and Miriam fed them with her stories and her affection for them. And when the day's story telling was over, she and Jonathan would talk, and Jonathan would describe things to her. At least some of the descriptions were true.

"At night," he said, "if it is warm enough, I come out of the caves and lie on the rough grass and look up in to the sky. Do you remember stars, Miriam?"

"No. I'm not sure I ever saw stars."

So Jonathan tried to describe the night sky for her. He described sunrise and sunset. And what came to be almost the most pleasant, he described her to herself. His description matched Esther's, and she began to believe that they knew more about the way she looked than her family did. She walked with her head high, hand on Samson.

One day when Esther was busy with one of her travellers, and Miriam was walking towards the Hill of Caves, she heard the sound of running feet, and then Jonathan's voice called her name.

"Miriam! Miriam!" He rushed up to her panting and flung his arms about her and kissed her on the cheek. She recoiled. It was Jonathan who made sure that she was never touched, who kept the curious fingers of the children from coming near her.

"It's all right!" Jonathan cried in a loud, glad voice. "I am healed! I am clean!" Again he took her in his arms, holding her to him, his words falling over each other in their hurry as he told her about a teacher who was walking through the countryside with his disciples, working miracles. "I went to find him, and I cried out to him to have mercy on me, and I was healed, I was made whole! I have not always told you the truth about the way I am. Miriam, but now I would like you to see me. I will take you to the Master and he will heal you."

In the circle of Jonathan's arms Miriam began to tremble. "He will make me not blind?"

"He will make you to see, and you won't need to wear that pretty bit of ribbon over your eyes any longer." With one hand he moved the silken bandage from her eyes; then the fingers of his other hand tightened on her arm.

Miriam asked in a low and angry voice, "Can he do that kind of a miracle? I don't believe it." She tied the delicate bandage over her eyes again.

"Miriam, my feet were raw and bleeding flesh. If I was often the last when the word came that you had reached the rock, it was because it took me so long to limp over to you. And now I am made whole. I can run and leap and dance with any man. Come! The Master is an hour's walk away. We'll have to hurry."

They walked quickly along the dusty road, Samson prancing along beside them and barking with pleasure. Jonathan continued to talk, to urge Miriam into belief. The heat of the sun beat against them, but Miriam felt cold.

They passed under the shadow of the gates of the neighbouring village. Miriam could feel the buildings about her, hanging over the narrow street. In what she sensed was a courtyard she could hear the murmurings and rustlings of a crowd of people. Jonathan led her through them, pushing and shoving, until there was a space.

"Master!" he cried. "I didn't thank you! but I give you my life, and I have brought you Miriam to heal."

There was a hush over the crowd. Miriam's hands were very cold and her heart beat wildly. Jonathan pushed her forwards, and then hands touched her.

A voice spoke, said "Miriam," and she was more wholly herself than she had ever thought possible. Then the voice said, "Daughter, be of good cheer. Thy sins be forgiven thee." The hands rested lightly on her shoulders and she felt the weight being lifted from them.

The silk was taken from her eyes, and then she heard Jonathan's flat voice, "Master, her eyes—"

The voice came, strong, with a hint of laughter. "My son, why do you think evil in your heart? Which do you think is easier? To say 'thy sins be forgiven thee,' or 'see'?"

Jonathan was silent. There was a low murmur from the crowd. Miriam waited. At last Jonathan's voice came, strong and clear. "It doesn't matter. I love her anyhow."

Now the laughter came. Much as Miriam loved Esther's bubbles of joy, this laughter was the most radiant thing she had ever heard, and she, too, broke into laughter. Then the voice said, "But that ye may know that the Son of man hath power on earth to forgive sins, I say unto thee that the scales shall drop from thine eyes. Receive thy sight."

Now the weight was entirely lifted from Miriam's shoulders. The air around her felt incredibly pure and light. She no longer bore a burden. She waited, smiling into the darkness.

"But Master—" Jonathan cried.

Miriam turned towards his voice. "But I see, Jonathan. I see as I never saw before, even when my eyes saw."

The voice spoke again. "Jonathan, you will come with me. I have work for you. And Miriam will go back where she is needed, as she is, to Esther the harlot and the lepers. Will you not, daughter?"

"Yes, Lord," Miriam said, "for I am healed."

The crowd made way for her as she turned and left, Samson guiding her.

This is again the one hundred and first miracle that Jesus did, when he was come out of Judea into Galilee.

Joanne Greenberg

In the introduction to another story, I briefly mentioned co-creation. I think I first came on the term in a book by Madeleine L'Engle and it is one of those ideas which has the power to upset all of our safe little categories. There is a responsibility and a duty inherent in co-creation, but there is also immense privilege. Gradually, as I began to explore the concept, words I had heard all my life began to take on new meaning: we are each special and unique, called into being for a purpose; we are not interchangeable.

And then one day came the realization that I—you—each of us—is called into being deliberately to make a difference. Our specific vocations may vary; our particular circumstances, our heredity and environment, will certainly vary, but we are all here to make a difference. We are needed. It is frightening to know that what I do here, now, today, may—in fact, quite probably, does—make a difference in some life far removed from mine. There is no way to describe the mixture of awe and humility and bubbling joy that that realization brought with it. My words, my actions, these stories may touch someone somewhere in a way none of us could ever have imagined: a dream may be born, a connection made, a laugh shared.

Actions have consequences, many of which we cannot see. I find that frightening, yes . . . but also exhilarating. My life rests not only in my hands, but in yours. Like climbers on a rope, we are linked together in life and in death.

· Joanne Greenberg ·

CERTAIN DISTANT SUNS

The planning of the Passover Seder was a tradition in our family. My mother and three aunts, dressed in their best, would go downtown. They would conduct their deliberations at a fancy restaurant over drinks, and this included a complete springtime going-over of every other member of the family. Mother usually returned from these sessions snapping with vigor and virtue, but on March 12, 1970, she came home later than usual, slammed the door, slammed into the kitchen, and began to fix supper with a lethal whacking of pots. "Bessie has refused!" she cried to us over a half-cooked, half-burnt meal. "There are four sisters. Each one gives the Seder every fourth year. This is Bessie's year, and she has refused."

"Is something the matter with Abe?" my father asked.

"No! She has the house, the health, the time, and the money. Those are requirements. The rest is her own headache, not a family matter. Not, when it comes down to it, a religious matter; not a requirement!"

In the end we found out that Aunt Bessie, in the fifty-sixth year of her life and three weeks before the Seder, had stopped believing in God.

Had we been Hasidim, Bessie's loss of faith might have been the prelude to one of their thrilling lawsuits against the Almighty.

59

Had we been Orthodox, her denial would have been the occasion for breast-beating and bowed heads, but we were then as we are now: modern American Jews, tangled in compromise, passing the past and the heritage hand to hand like a hot potato and wincing with pain between the toss and the catch. Our belief or nonbelief was different from Bessie's only in degree. She hadn't weakened us spiritually; she had only annoyed us, and she had broken the solidarity of the family. Minnie gave the Seder. Eyebrows were raised but no voices. Bessie stayed away; her husband and children came and sat stiff and uncomfortable at the table. She was a stronger presence there than Elijah. My mother sighed and shook her head. I was nineteen; I thought it was wonderful.

As time passed, we learned to live around Bessie's peculiarity. To all secular family events she came as generously and happily as before. Presents on birthdays, soup in sickness. She would ring the bell with a kind of snap— "Bessie's ring"—and would hurry in as though propelled from behind, her wiry hair unkempt and flying, her plucked eyebrows drawn on again in black pencil with a perpetually upshot line, her voice rich as a singer's (although she couldn't carry a tune—too impatient, I think). When the High Holy Days were glimpsed over the heat-watering horizon of summer and plans were made for the sharing of dinners and the attendance at services, Bessie dwindled to the point of disappearance. As the Lord rose in the web of the year, Aunt Bessie diminished only to reappear when the holy days were past.

The name of God disappeared from her lips. I was the first to notice this—such secular usages that we don't even remember Whose Name it is: Good-bye, Goddammit, for God's sake, Lord knows. No hint of Him. Not any of His Names. She did not tell us what had led to this loss of belief or the more bizarre divorcing of herself from the most common associations with the Name. To my knowledge, no one asked her. Which is, for us, unusual. Ours is a family that allows few secrets and no evasions. We are skilled and merciless trackers. We corner the secret-keepers at funerals and feasts and drive the diffident to the wall. We will not wait for the truth to out; we hector it forth with whatever force is necessary. Except, because we are Jews, for that most subtle of links, broken and rewoven a hundred times a day: belief. We did not examine the broken link.

And Bessie was getting along spendidly without the Lord. She traveled lighter, unburdened of the baggage of belief. We milled away at our compromises, grinding them now coarser, now finer; we were caught surprised as holidays loomed up suddenly from ambush to overwhelm us. We blurred the Sabbath and felt guilty; we violated the laws of kashrut and felt defensive. Bessie sailed past it all and never looked better. Her house was as spotless as ever. The houseplants thrived under her hands; her soufflés fell not, neither did her custards fail. The rezoning of Martin Park stopped four blocks from her house, raising its value by a third.

Occasionally, my mother would mention some religious matter in Bessie's presence and would give one of her significant looks in Bessie's direction. Since belief was not truly an issue—Bessie was incontrovertibly and immutably a Jew by Jewish Law—all that remained for discussion was her uncooperativeness. Unfortunately, Bessie, in secular matters, was remarkably cooperative and the soul of considerate sisterliness. When anyone needed help Bessie was there, and when she heard that my parents were going to the banquet for the national-headquarters people in my father's firm, she came running over with Great Grandma's garnets.

I turned the mammoth ring over in my hand. "Try on the earrings, darling," Bessie said to me. "They're just right with your coloring."

"No thanks," I said quickly and handed the things back. "The ring alone would slow anybody down."

"I'll wear them for the evening," my mother said to Bessie, "and I'll return them this weekend."

"Keep them as along as you like," Bessie said. "Since I gave up the safety-deposit box they're only in my way."

"You're not changing banks again, are you?" (Bessie was a sucker for the free premiums.)

"Which bank is it this time, Aunt Bessie, the one on Tyler Avenue?"

"No," Bessie said cheerfully. "I've decided that I really don't believe in all that anymore, the savings and the safety and the capital and the principal and the interest and the stocks and the bonds and the balances. I've closed my account in the banks and turned in my charge cards. Money is real. Money in the hand is real—coins and bills. The rest I don't believe in, and I don't think I ever did, really. What's a check, after all, but a promise—mine, the bank's. Me, I know, but the bank? You know how quick those tellers change down there; you don't even get to know their names before they leave. Them I should trust?"

"But if you can't think of the convenience," my mother cried, "think of the danger. Money in the house, money in your purse. Think of fire and theft. What if—"

"What if," Bessie said and waved her hand, dismissing it all, "what if no one could be sure of anything!"

Had we been Hasidim we would have waited the lightning stroke or a case of boils. Had we been Orthodox, we would have searched for the first faint whiff of corruption in her, some hint of moral or ethical disintegration, perhaps for symptoms, physical or psychiatric, that would show us that she was despairing or alienated—not that she had ceased believing in banks, but that she seemed actively to be calling down destruction upon herself, a condition from which Jews have always turned in abhorrence. We make poor martyrs and worse ascetics. As it was, we could only wait and watch without knowing what we should wait and watch for.

The months passed. Bessie's housekeeping money went in a coffee can. The stock dividends from the family business were cashed and put in other coffee cans. The IRS got a mailing envelope crammed with bills representing their dividend of her dividends. Bills were paid in person. Neither did fire strike, nor criminals spring from the shadows upon her as my father predicted. In my thoughts, Bessie began to fill a larger space than the other aunts. I saw her as younger, happier, freer than they. The petty details that were weighing my mother down year after year—rules and laws, record keeping, busywork—did not touch Bessie. She had fought free of them, and her courage was keeping her young and heroic and outlined against the family background in sharper relief. When the consciousness-raising seminars came to our school and I sat and heard my "sisters" talk about the heroic women of the past, none of those women were Jews. Sojourner Truth and Harriet Tubman and the Quaker ladies of concern and the early defenders of women's rights held sway, but I was sure that had the underground railway gone through our time and place, Bessie would have been one of the conductors.

Spring came and the women of our family became narrow-eyed and diligent. Roach paste was painted around the bathroom pipes and in the corners. Stiff-jointed ladies bent themselves double to clean the sinister places behind the sinks and toilets and plotted elaborate stratagems against beetles, ants, and silverfish. Bessie knelt at no open cabinets, genuflected beneath no plumbing. As the ground warmed and the hundred million flies of the new generation remembered us, screens went up in all the windows of the neighborhood. Except one. Fly killer in sprays, bricks, strips, candles, flares, and lightbulbs appeared in every shopping cart and was stocked in the newly cleaned cabinets of every dwelling. Except one. Fear of disease, plague, filth, and corruption (ritual and actual) haunted the half sleep of every householder. Except one. Bessie had given up germs.

"My God! Bessie," my mother cried, "you won't last the summer! Flies in the food—every disease known to man!"

"Germs is a theory," Bessie answered with her usual vigor. "It says so in the books—the germ theory. I stopped believing in the theory, and I won't let it bother me anymore. Think about the people in the olden days. Did they use fly spray? Did they worry about pollution and disease all the time? No. They lived until they were ninety-five, some of them, in the middle of cities that teemed with rats and flies. Show me a rat as big as I am and I'll be afraid of it. Show me a germ and I'll believe in it all."

"In a microscope—"

"I'll live in a microscope and I'll believe in the germs there."

"My aunt is at one, in harmony, with the natural order," I said to my sisters at a meeting. "My sister is crazy," my mother said. "What bad things have happened to me?" Bessie asked. "Am I sick? Have plagues fallen on me? You see that I am fine—better than ever. I sleep better and eat better because I don't have to worry about supernatural punishments or money or sickness."

And it was true. The cataclysms predicted by my parents were not forthcoming. The flies in Bessie's house came in no greater numbers than those in ours in spite of all our care and her uncaring. I know, because after making a bet with my father, I counted them for him and all the family prophets of disaster who seemed obscurely disappointed that Bessie and Abe lived on unafflicted. In early August Bessie put up six quarts of pickles without steam scouring the crocks or boiling the jars. Mold formed and floated serenely on the tops of the crocks, but when Bessie skimmed it away, I found the pickles delicious and unspoiled. And Bessie wasn't sick. No colds or flu or aching joints or fevers or chills or swollen ears or congestions, inflammations, or eruptions. She was healthier than she had ever been, her skin clearer, her face less lined. She seemed lighter, too, freer, head up in the street even in bad weather while most of the other women in the neighborhood passed by, eyes down, bodies hunched against the rain, frightened by the cough of the passenger next to them on the bus, the dirty nails of the shopkeeper, the sneeze of the postman. Bessie's fearlessness was wonderful to me, and it showed even brighter against the nervousness and hypochondria of the rest of the family. After seeing Bessie, how much poorer and sicker the rest of them looked to me! Aunt Dorothy was afraid of being mugged in the street, Aunt Minnie of what she called "getting a condition" in fear of which she marshaled a pharmacopeia sufficient to supply a city. My mother was terrified of being caught somewhere without any money and died night after night in a hundred old-age homes without the dime for a phone call out. I seldom argued Bessie's case to the family—it only made my father laugh at her more and my mother shake her head. I showed my loyalty by visiting her often and my courage by staying for supper. In my parents' house dark and evil forces went to work on any food left out of a refrigerator for thirty seconds. Bessie's casual attitude was exciting to me. Would there be souring? Sickness? Plague? In a life insufficiently precarious, I felt I was a hostage to comfort. Bessie's danger was a tonic to my soul.

We had one brief cooling, a hiatus in our relationship. It happened when Ray and I, bowing to pressure from both our families, consented to stop living together and get married. Once the decision was made we found ourselves happy with it, eager for the status we had always ridiculed, the granting of full man-and-womanhood to us by our families. We even enjoyed helping to plan the wedding. When I told Bessie, she beamed and invited us over for a meal. Bessie's husband Abe worked long hours at his store. We seldom saw him, but Bessie promised he would be there for the dinner and for my wedding. "Surely you'll be there too . . . ."

But the wedding was to be a Jewish wedding—a religious ceremony—and Bessie must have known it. I was the foolish one. I had supposed that because it was to be my wedding, because I was her favorite niece, she would come. I had always admired her stand, her refusal to compromise with what she had no belief in, yet when it came to me, I wanted her love to suspend her disbelief. She stayed away. Abe came. He had an easygoing attitude toward Bessie, which was lucky under the circumstances. But I was hurt and Bessie knew it. She had sent us a huge chafing dish. It was the gift I had known it would be—exuberant, impractical, no compromise. I set it up on top of the kitchen cabinet in our small apartment against the day when we would entertain on such a scale. When I next saw her she was so free of guilt or explanation or reproach that I couldn't really stay angry—my anger seemed unreal. Her absence at my wedding seemed unreal. I soon stopped believing in it.

I did not see my relatives for a while. I assumed that they were standing in the positions in which I had left them, unchanging. It is enough of a shock that the people we see daily change before our eyes; it is unthinkable that the rest of reality is so far beyond our control. One day in April my mother brought over my old summer clothes and some of her own to alter on my machine. We work well together on projects like that, chatting companionably over our decisions, planning the alterations for the things we keep, fitting and refitting. Our tastes are similar, and we laugh and remember the days and events at which we wore this outfit or that. I had been looking forward to a peaceful afternoon. I had taken off from work for it. There was a nice lunch made.

But when I saw her at the door the pleasure went out of the day. She looked worried and frightened. I helped her unload the boxes she had brought from the car. "What's the matter?"

"Later, later," she said.

When we were upstairs, I asked again.

"It's Bessie. It's gone too far this time—Bessie has given up electricity."

I think I laughed. "No one 'gives up' electricity. A person who 'gives up' electricity has no neural function. That person is dead."

"Stop being childish," my mother said angrily. "Bessie is alive enough, but she has stopped believing in electricity, and strange things are happening in that house!"

"What strange things? What does Uncle Abe say?" She was too upset to tell me any more. I could see that she was frightened and a little angry and also that she was angry at me. I had encouraged Bessie with my admiration, goaded her on from one selfishness to another with my shining-eyed approval. She had played to my youth and eagerness; perhaps it is easy for a middle-aged woman to fall into such a trap, to forget that she is middle-aged, too old for nonsense, for beliefs or disbeliefs that put a strain on the family. "Should I go and see her?" I asked before my mother left.

"You might as well," my mother said, as though she meant, "See what you have started."

But I hadn't started it and I wasn't to blame. Could I help it if I admired idealism, honesty, and independence? Could I help it if these were Bessie's virtues and if they are also virtues of the young? I admired her still, I would help and encourage her if I could. The next day I called in sick and went over to Bessie's house.

Bessie's street was a quietly decaying side street of two-family houses with small back gardens and great old trees. Going up the slightly tilted steps I thought I heard the TV with its warm, male drone. Most of the sets in this neighborhood were on during the day. The neighborhood was old, the street full of widows who filled their houses with the sounds of genial, sympathetic men—the suffering doctors of soap operas and the spruce hosts of game shows. If Bessie wasn't using electricity anymore, perhaps the sound was coming from the Galindas in the other half of the house. I rang Bessie's harsh, old-fashioned bell. There was no sound. Oh, yes, electricity. I knocked. After a minute or so I heard Bessie's footsteps going from the worn rug to the foyer floor. Then the door opened.

I studied her for changes. There was something, although I couldn't put my finger on it, and I cursed the curiosity that made me want to peer in through her defenses. Her hair was standing up around her head as usual, her movements were brisk, and she greeted me in that rich, loud voice of hers. "Come on in; you look wonderful! I've been fixing up Danny's old bedroom and I could use a break."

"I thought I heard voices in here when I was at the door," I said. There was silence now. Bessie's face clouded. "I like a little company when I work, that's all. Your mother has been blabbing about it all over town, and my big-mouth sister Minnie, too." She had hurried into the kitchen and was filling a kettle at the sink. I saw her hand tremble a little. It could have been anger at my mother and Aunt Minnie, but there was something else on her face, an expression I couldn't read. "What if a person wants to hear some programs—have some company while she works! What's so wrong about that?" She was really upset now and al- most in tears—not tears of sorrow but of anger and frustration.

"Aunt Bessie, what's the matter?" I cried.

"Well, if you really want to know. I'll show you, but please don't make more of it than there really is!" She took me into the living room.

It was a modest room; Uncle Abe worked hard but he was not very successful. The furniture came mostly from my grandparents' house. Serviceable, Bessie called it. In the corner was an old TV, black-and-white. As I looked at it, I remembered the furor that Bessie had made when my parents had finally gone to color. Un- cle Abe liked this set, which he had gotten with the twenty-one- inch screen when the rest of us still had nineteen-inch. Now Bessie sometimes called herself "the only sister without color." I noticed that the set was unplugged. Bessie turned the knob. "What do you want to see?" she asked.

"What's on?" I smiled, thinking that she was perhaps going to tell a joke.

"What do you want to see?" she asked impatiently. "Pick some- thing you want to see."

"I don't know—you pick something."

Medical shows. Doctors. In color—brilliant, clear color. Transfixed, I saw "Medic," "Ben Casey," "Dr. Kildare," "The Nurses." I saw brain operations, heart seizures, epidural hemato- mas. The crises poured out upon us without snow, flopover, or distortion. All the doctors spoke in Yiddish. All the nurses looked familiar; I realized that they all resembled our family. Midway through a lateral-transorbital-shunt procedure, I asked Bessie why, except for medical terms, Dr. Ben Casey wasn't speaking English. "Shush!" she said. "Wait for the commercial!"

During the commercial she told me some of the limitations of her set. "Radio shows I can get on TV also, but then I don't get a picture. Fibber McGee I get in the daytime, never in Yiddish. Benny and Berle I get in Yiddish. The doctors I can get in either language, but they are more sympathetic in Yiddish. I always like to have Dr. Ben Casey and Marcus Welby in Yiddish."

"I don't understand how you do it—how it happens," I cried. "Especially when nothing is plugged in."

"Well," she said, "I don't believe in electricity—in wires carrying power from a waterfall somewhere, but I believe in color and I believe in Ben Casey and the good work he does. I believe in Fibber McGee and his closet and I believe in Jack Benny, how stingy he is and how he tries to stay thirty-nine years old. Oh, I know no doctor could be like Marcus Welby, but I believe in it anyway. A person shouldn't have to accept anything he doesn't believe in."

"Can you get the iron and the toaster to work without plugging them in?"

"Nothing will work but this. Still, people were cleaning their houses and washing their clothes years before electricity. I clean in the old way, and Abe takes the clothes out to—"

As we spoke a black-and-white figure came on the screen. I saw it for only a second before Bessie leaped up from the couch where we sat and turned off the set with a curse. The picture did not go away immediately but went black-red like an afterimage from the sun, and slowly the figure, arm raised as though to defend or to exhort, faded soundlessly from the set. Bessie watched it with a look of bitterness I had never seen on her face in all the years I had known her. "What was that?" I asked uncomfortably.

"A commercial!" she hissed. I did not dare ask any more.

Ours is a family of large egos. We gossip because we feel our smallest news must be as fascinating to everyone else as it is to us.

Deliverymen and storekeepers know every grandchild's new tooth, every symptom. Each day the family's vital signs are broadcast to everyone who will listen. This habit fooled me into thinking that we could not keep a secret. I was wrong. If you want to keep a secret, bury it in talk. Neither the family, the children, nor even my husband, Ray, knew about Bessie's arcane gift. We who shared the secret had a never-mentioned horror of reporters, psychic investigators, universities, parapsychologists, and all the other interested (self- or otherwise) persons besieging the family to test and probe and question, document, report, explore, explode, destroy. Luckily, the lights worked in the house—Bessie believed in light. They had a gas stove, and she cooked in the usual way. Thank God for small favors.

Sometimes women in my consciousness-raising group would ask me about Bessie. In the past I had used her as an example of a woman heroically above the demeaning adjustments that threaten us all. The group, still fragile and unsure, wanted Founders, Roots, History. These women saw in Bessie, or in my stories of Bessie, a "resource," as they called it, something as natural as a mineral, as usable as water. And suddenly I was frightened and silent. I said she was sick. It was a good excuse. Illness is not part of the image of the liberated woman. It reminds young people of dependence, real and sham, of limitations. Of compromise.

And then I got sick. Suddenly the sure things—health, strength, that organs would do their work silently and automatically—all these things were suddenly not sure at all. There was dizziness and weakness, sudden sweats and sudden chills. "A renal crisis" the doctor said. In essence I had begun to poison myself. I went to the hospital.

After several false starts, the treatment took effect. The weakness drew away slowly, but I was now on notice that anywhere, at any time, any one of a thousand ills could fall on me like an eagle falling upon a feeding rabbit, could take me and transform me in moments into an invalid, a person not myself, a person at the mercy of blood-washing machines, pumps, tubes, and wires.

It was more than a renal crisis. It was crisis of belief exactly the opposite of Bessie's . . . where was Bessie?

"Where's Aunt Bessie? Why hasn't she come?"

"You always said you hated that in our family, everyone checking off who sent things and who came and who called and what excuses people gave—"

"I'm not doing that; I only want to see her—I need to see her."

"Cousin Grace has been here almost every day—"

"Cousin Grace is not Bessie. I can't stand one more description of Cousin Grace's canals—she doesn't visit the sick, she haunts them. Where is Aunt Bessie?"

Had I not been weak and ill I would not have seen my mother's discomfort. Skilled cornerers make skilled prevaricators, but my mother couldn't play that game now. You can lie to people; not to machines. I was half machine. My mother was stumped. She came close to the bed. "Don't tell Ray—" she whispered. I think I must have gone very pale.

"What is it, Ma?"

"Bessie can't come to see you. She would if she could. She can't leave the house at all anymore. Bessie has stopped believing in gravity."

As soon as I was out of the hospital I went to see her. I was still weak, still separated by a great unmeasured gulf from the world, from anyone who has no serious doubts about rising whole the next morning and who tranquilly says "I will come," "I will go," as though he could make such promises.

I was shocked at the change in Bessie's house. It was autumn, and the corpses of dried leaves were banked against the sides of the steps in little heaps. Bessie would never have allowed that had something not been terribly wrong. The outside of her house had always been immaculate. In a neighborhood of two-family houses the facades, walks, steps, and doorways are a matter of intense rivalry among the housewives. I had grown up hearing Bessie mutter about "the slut" three houses down "who didn't sweep until noon, practically." Now, all down the row, the clean steps of the other houses mocked her, and I shivered.

Looking up into Bessie's parlor window, I saw that the off-white curtains were limp and dingy. I began to formulate reasons for my visit. This in itself made me nervous. Excuses had never been needed. Aunt Bessie's house had always been as free to me as my own, sometimes more so, while I was growing up and often at odds with my mother. I wanted to run up the stairs freely and eagerly as I had countless times before to give and take confidences and laughter over cake and milk. But I stopped at the leaf-strewn steps, uncertain and listening. Maybe the TV would be on—"Our Gal Sunday" as a Polish immigrant girl speaking a sweet Litvak Yiddish, or Dr. Marcus Welby, comforting in the mother tongue. There was silence. Only the accusing leaves whispered and rustled in the warm afternoon. I rang the bell and remembering again, knocked, feeling like a stranger.

I didn't hear the familiar steps. Instead, the door swung open and I saw nothing. I stood at the opening. "Aunt Bessie?"

"Come in!" a voice hissed—from where I could not tell. I stepped into the dark foyer, light-blinded. It was a while before I saw her.

She lay prone in the air above me, hand on the knob. When the door closed, the wind of its closing blew her up and into a lazy somersault, back and forth. She banked and turned and slowly brought herself upright to face me. Her skin was gray. "Come into the kitchen," she said. "It's better in the kitchen." With a kind of swimming stroke she breasted her way before me. She had not greeted me or looked to see if I was well. She hadn't smiled. Her eyes hadn't lit up at my presence. I sat down at the table. Bessie bobbed in the air beside me, up and down, now oblique to the right, now overbalancing to the left—never still. It embarrassed me to look and, even more, to turn my head away. I gave a quick glance around the once-familiar kitchen.

For some people it might have been a passable kitchen before the morning cleanup. For Bessie in her present condition it must have been an agony. Crumbs lay in the corners and were picked out by the afternoon sun that shone in through the dusty window. Dishes stood in the sink, and there was a film of grease on the range top. She looked around at it all with a glare of disgust. "It's a nightmare!" she said bitterly, "a nightmare!"

"Oh, Aunt Bessie!" I cried.

Two tears formed in her eyes. She put her hand up to her face and then shook her head. The tears leaped away to hang in the air in two large drops and then fell with a splat to the floor. The motion of shaking her head had brought her up out of the chair, which she had been holding onto, and over into a roll from which she righted herself after several minutes. She sighed deeply but didn't say anything. Her situation was so unreal and her misery so real I cast around for anything I could offer to bring things under our control. "Men in space—" I said, "the astronauts—those men learn to adjust. They develop all kinds of ways of making peace with their condition—" (Why had I said that? It sounded like something a rabbi would say).

"How?" she cried back at me in a kind of bitter triumph. "Lead shoes? Weights? I've tried them all. As soon as I put anything on me, it becomes weightless, too."

"Maybe someone could come in to help—until you get the feel of things—"

"Who? Who would come in to help a bouncing woman, a floating woman, a double- and triple-flip woman, and not go blabbing it all over town! Am I crazy? Do I want crowds at the windows watching me loop-the-loop? Abe helps—he shops a little now—your mother, Minnie, Dotty, and Cousin Clara, but I can't go out at all. I'm trapped in this house, and I can't stand to stay in here and look at this—this *pigsty*!" Once again tears formed in her eyes and wouldn't roll out until she tossed her head and went head over heels in recoil.

I had nothing to give her. I was unequipped for keeping company in grief, for weeping over what couldn't be changed. My training was all for answers, kindly and helpful suggestions, practical dispositions, for tactics, marches, petitions, and demands for redress. Surely somewhere was the solution, that certain, helpful thing, that method, formula, or hint that no one had thought of before and that would seem so right when I said it.

"Maybe," I started . . . .

"Do you know that when I make the bed I go up with the sheets? When I turn over in bed I turn for half an hour until I get sick, and if I'm sick enough to throw up I have to hang on or I fly away?"

"At least you don't *have* to go out. Uncle Abe does the shopping. Everyone is helping. I'll help too. You've got the radio and the TV in that wonderful color—all the shows that ever were and every movie you ever saw. Maybe you could start to make your own movies, to be creative by—"

Bessie leaned close and whispered, and the force of her whispering caused her to bob up and down. "I can't watch TV anymore, or radio. I can't because of the commercials!"

"The commercials—when I saw them on your set that day they were no different from—"

"That was before!" Bessie hissed. "It's all different now! You think the sponsor would let such a chance go by, a helpless woman trapped in the house like I am?" She looked down at me, pinched, old, aggrieved. The energy of her hissing had pushed her up and away until she lay prone in the air again, near the ceiling. I found myself remembering the authority of her tread, the vigor of her ring. It was less than a year ago that her presence everywhere was heralded with so much certainty. Now there wouldn't even be a footfall.

"Everybody hates commercials." Reasonable and lost and thinking that if only I were more reasonable I would not be so lost, I said, "They drive me mad, especially when they interrupt something. We all—"

"No! No!" And she flailed her arms in impatience. In space all Italians, Jews, and Spaniards will be punished and the hand-mute Saxons will be vindicated by the God of Newton, who hates all wasted motion. Bessie began to spin and turn. Not humbled but enraged, she cried, "Go turn on the set, Mrs. Smarty, and see for yourself!" Hopelessly I went into the parlor and turned on the unplugged set.

The picture came on immediately. Bessie's black-and-white console erupted in luscious color again. It was a movie called *Red Garters* with Rosemary Clooney. There was dancing and gaiety. There were lots of songs. No one spoke Yiddish in this one, but it was just the thing to raise the spirits—everyone was pretty or witty or graceful. The color was richer than any I had ever seen on TV. I called Aunt Bessie in to watch. Surely this couldn't hurt her. She came swimming into the parlor disconsolately, and for a while we watched the dancing and the music. Once or twice I saw her smiling a little. After about fifteen minutes there was a station break. The movie stopped abruptly, and the call letters RUACH-TV came on the screen in black-and-white. I turned to Bessie. "What station is that? I never heard of it before, and there's a picture of a shofar in the background."

"Turn it off," she said dully. A commercial or announcement of some kind began.

It had obviously been staged in the studio by rank amateurs. A slight, bent Hasidic Jew stood uncomfortably on one foot and then on the other. He took off his glasses and wiped them and then held them dangling from his hand. He could not have been an actor in costume. The clothes were too obviously his, although nothing matched—pants too short, sleeves too long, the beard bushy as though he had a chin full of gray foam. He spoke in Yiddish very slowly and haltingly, but it was a Yiddish unfamiliar to me, and the word I knew here and there gave me no clue. Bessie was floating up over me, hovering in the air. "What's he saying?" I asked, looking up at her. She sighed. "This is the sad one. At least he's better than the angry one, the one who squints."

"Yes, but what's he saying?"

She began to interpret. " 'I'm pleading with all the people,' he says, 'in the vast television audience, not to renounce the universe along with the Master of the Universe, if for some reason they find it necessary to renounce Him. I realize,' he says, 'that in every relationship a certain amount of resentment builds up over the years and that this is especially true in regard to mankind and the Master of the Universe, since the relationship is so . . . so one-sided.' He says, 'I beg you, all of you, not to stop discussing the Master of the Universe, even if you can no longer praise Him. If it be in anger or despair or even, God forbid, in ridicule, keep His Name aloud in your mouths. It is possible that certain distant suns are powered by the mention of His Name.' "

The movie began again; Bessie was crying and so was I, but I didn't want to turn off the set. When the angry one came on, the one with the squint, Bessie shook her fist at him and was pushed softly against the wall, bouncing slightly back and forth. There she stayed, answering his angry incomprehensible questions.

"You left Him!" the Rabbi shouted at last, in English. "You sent Him away, abandoned Him, abandoned your part of Him, a part that can never be replaced!"

"I stopped believing in Him, what could I do?" Bessie shouted back.

"Foolish woman, a soul goes in and out of belief a hundred times a day. Belief is too fragile to weigh a minute on. You stopped running after Him, looking for Him, struggling with Him. Even His Laws you turned from!"

"If I did, why did He take it, why did He walk away like a whipped child? Is He no stronger than a fifty-year-old woman?"

"How can His relationship with you be any stronger than you are yourself? You think He made you for the fun of it—without needing you?"

"He let it happen, that's all I know! He didn't fight back. A *mensch* fights back!"

Starr Luteri

We are all special because we have each been called into being by name. We matter; we are unique and every one of us is blessed with an individual vocation, but if we are like most people, it is not enough to be special, we want to be more special *than,* more talented *than,* prettier *than.* "Ceyx" is a frightening story because any one of us might have fallen into the trap Marcia falls into; we are none of us free of our little prides and the tiny inner voice that says, "You really are more special *than.* . . ."

Comparisons are a great breeding ground for evil; nothing helps the great Tempter more than dividing people, severing connections. When I am helped to see myself as more special than someone else, as slightly above or outside the laws that govern human relationships, I have put a wall between myself and the rest of humanity; I am fair game for the one who understands best the truth behind the phrase, "divide and conquer."

Miss Luteri has drawn the picture of a couple divided by the infinite, day-to-day failures in communication that beset us all. We all carry about with us old prejudices, old fears, old angers, that cloud our vision and make us unable to hear the needs of those we love. You may say, as I did, "If only Jack and Marcia had been able to talk, to share. . . ." Yes: if only. But "if only" requires a new way of looking at life. It requires that we put ourselves in one another's shoes, not only when we are feeling good, but when we are tired and grouchy and problem-ridden. "If only" requires that we give up our cherished roles and the ways they allow us to manipulate other people, and wake new to each day, born and reborn again. It requires us to look, really look, at life and to listen with the ears of the heart as well as the ears of the head. It is a challenge that brings a priceless reward: connectedness with the universe.

· Starr Luteri ·

CEYX

There is a progression in the meditative life. It is a life of learning; first, to become still, to enter into the recreating silence; second, to become disciplined, and allow the fragmentation of our minds to become focused. Finally, we learn to listen, outwardly and inwardly, until we receive the revelation that brings to us the divine breath of peace. Above all, we must learn to listen.

Marcia set the book down and turned off the reading lamp, then sat with eyes closed, feet together, hands resting lightly in her lap. Night sounds crept around the house, marking the movement of time. The children murmured in their dreams, stretching and growing toward their own images of silence. Jack rolled over on the other side of the bed and pulled the light summer quilt closer around himself. Marcia heard none of these. The sounds of the river were in her ears.

The wooded slope on which she stood rose to a rocky crest before joining the mountain which continued climbing upward far to her left; from beyond the crest came sounds of the river. Marcia started through the undergrowth and fern, covering several hundred yards in less than a moment. When she reached the rocks, she found them velveted with mosses and tiny flowering plants. Clambering over these boulders in the physical world would be bruising work, but here she leapt from one outcropping to another with little effort. She pulled up onto the highest rock, the wind lifting her hair from her shoulders and mist washing her skin in a sparkling spray. The sheer cliffs still rose above her on the left, continuing in a half circle to the opposite side of a narrow chasm into which fell a gleaming arch of water, diving from some point in the invisible heights above. The sun was rising or setting beyond the mountain; around the precipice streamed impossible shades of crimson and gold. Lower in the valley the river tossed back gleams of colored light as it swirled and bounded between cliffs and boulders until at last it vanished across the gulf. Colors merged, forming themselves into twin crescents of iridescent brilliance, and the tumbling roar of the waters became the voice of the Angel: "Follow me."

Marcia turned her back to the light and started after the Angel, who was already some distance away, moving down the course of the river. Her guide maintained his distance, but never too far for her to lose sight of the gossamer iridescence of his wings through the leaves. It occurred to her that the powerful spirit wore no clothes; his huge form moved unencumbered, at ease among the rocks and trees. Where they finally came to rest, the gorge opened out into a green meadow surrounded by birch and willow.

The river was flowing here in a wide stream; it played over the grass and slid in and out behind hillocks of lilies and iris until it disappeared through hedges at the border of the lawn. This might have been a botanical garden sown by a gardener gone mad: roses, dahlias, and peonies tumbled over one another, while miniature daisies and poppies rioted in the grass. Every color of the rainbow fall was repeated in this field, but magnified and tossed in magnificent disarray. The floral odors were so thick and heady that Marcia was nearly overcome; she wanted to laugh and sing, or else to lie down and sleep—she did not know which.

"What river is this?" She startled at her own voice.

"It is the Lethe." Her guide moved to the edge of the stream and knelt to the crystal water. She followed and stared through the glassy depths where they could see grasses and flowers waving in the current, twin of those waving in the meadow breeze. "We shall follow it to its end, you and I, to the consummation of perfect joy." As he spoke, the Angel's face lit with a brightness so intense that she covered her own face with her arms. The joyous fire seared her forehead, her breasts, her arms, and then it was gone. When she dropped her hands she was staring at the pillow and the alarm clock was ringing.

"The consummation of perfect joy." The promise was its own fulfillment. Marcia was humming while she rolled out biscuits for Jack and the boys, set out a bowl of low-calorie cereal for herself, then hustled down to the basement to toss a T-shirt and shorts into the dryer: Jack liked his linens fresh and warm when he finished his shower. The morning routine continued like any other day: turn on the news, set coffee on the stove, pull together salami and cheese in case Jack needed to carry his lunch. Morning used to be the worst part of the day. Even if she managed every job on time, she appeared frazzled at the breakfast table, when Jack especially enjoyed seeing her fresh and pretty. This morning he ought to be pleased. She ran a comb through her curls and put on a hint of lipstick.

Two little boys followed their daddy down the steps. "Good morning, doll, where's my coffee?"

"It's on the table, hon. Did you put Davy on the toilet upstairs?"

Jack turned up the volume of the television. "Nope. That's your job. Daddies don't change diapers. Where's the butter? You always forget to get the butter out of the refrigerator in the morning, and then it's too hard to spread on the biscuits."

"Okay, I'll remember tomorrow," Marcia answered from the bathroom. Nothing could dampen her happiness this morning. The consummation of perfect joy. She sat down to her bowl of cereal and skim milk, only to bounce up again to find peanut butter and jelly and to pour Jack another cup of coffee. "Did you sleep well, hon?"

"No, I kept waking up. I think it's that new clock you've got at your side of the bed; it makes too much noise. I want you to get rid of that thing and find one that isn't so loud." Jack shoved his plate away and stretched back in the chair. "Did you have any time to pray this morning?"

It was a daily question which Marcia used to dread. "Yes, I prayed in bed, before you woke up."

"Good girl. What scripture did you read?"

That was unexpected. "Oh, I didn't study this morning, just prayed. I've got my group meeting this afternoon, and we always cover a chapter or so."

"Sounds fine, babe." Jack pulled on his sports coat and looked around for his briefcase. "Where did you put my . . . never mind, there it is. I don't need the lunch today, I'm meeting a client at noon." He kissed her on the forehead and started out the door. "Let's have pot roast for supper tonight."

"Oh, honey, the kids don't like pot roast and we just had it last Sunday."

"Well, you make the pot roast for me, and I'll pick up burgers and fries for the kids on my way home. How's that? Oh, by the way," he shut the door and came back into the room. "I noticed that you look very nice this morning." He took her by the wrists and pulled her against him. "What makes you so smiley, hm? What are you thinking about in that sweet little head of yours?"

Marcia was pleased so she answered truthfully, "The consummation of perfect joy."

"Sounds sexy to me." He wrapped her arms around his neck and spoke softly in her ear. "How about I come home early tonight, and you get the kids over to Grandma's, hm?"

Marcia disentangled her wrists and gently pushed him toward the door. "Go on, you're going to be late for work."

"All right, but I'm warning you. I'll be home early." He threw her the grin she knew so well, then paused again, halfway out the door. "You know, doll, I've been thinking. You've been happier lately, not so depressed. I get worried when you're depressed." A shadow of concern crossed his face, then melted into his mischievous grin. "I think maybe it's about time we talked about another baby."

Marcia watched from the door as he pulled out of the drive and drove down the street. Josh and Davy were squabbling over the TV; a box of Cheerios was spilled on the couch. She swept up the last of the cereal from the floor, and turned down the television before going upstairs to make the beds. Meditation had brought peace, after so many years of spiritual advice and loving condemnation had failed.

"Have you prayed about it?" Mrs. Creggle had asked at their prayer group meeting one day last spring, passing the donuts. Of course she had prayed, why else would she be asking them for help? But she could not explain how her prayers had no wings, but hung limp in the branches outside the window where she sat.

"Are you aware of any sin in your life?" Sara Miller spooned coffee creamer into her cup. "You know, it is possible to sin without realizing it, and sin will take away your joy."

"Perhaps the trouble lies in your relationship with Jack." Dorothy Classon was the pastor's wife and specialized in marital relationships. "If you are not in submission to your husband's authority, even in your attitude, you certainly cannot expect to be joyful."

Sophie Goddard came to the defense. "Dorothy, I really don't think that Marcia's problem has anything to do with her not being submissive to Jack." She reached across the coffee table and squeezed her friend's hand. "We've been close ever since we joined this group, and as far as I can see, Marica's just about the most submissive wife I know."

Helen Gussets blew her nose with a noisy snort into a green tissue. "Marcia, dear child, I want you to open your Bible and turn to First Thessalonians five, verse sixteen. That says, 'Rejoice, always.' Now turn to Second Corinthians thirteen, let's see, verse eleven. That says, 'Rejoice, be made complete, be com-

forted . . . . 'Dear girl, those are not requests, those are com-
mandments. Giving way to depression is disobeying the command
of God to rejoice!" Helen snapped her Bible shut. "What you
need to do is beg forgiveness for the sin of depression and submit
yourself to the discipline of the Lord,"

Sophie had followed Marcia home after the group broke up. "I
could tell that you were upset, and I don't blame you, not after
what Helen said." She picked up Davy and wiped his nose while
Marcia put the Bible and notebooks away. "You must not mind
her really, Marcia. Helen knows her chapter and verse, but when
it comes to understanding the spirit of the word, well, that just
isn't her gift."

"But she's probably right," Marcia had said. Davy jumped off
Sophie's lap and ran into the yard after his brother. "There it is,
right in Scripture."

"The Psalms say to clap your hands and shout unto the Lord;
when was the last time you saw Helen Gussets clapping her hands
in church?" It had worked—Marcia could not resist smiling at the
idea. "No, that's enough about Helen, I'm sure she means well.
What I want to talk about is you, and the feelings you shared with
us this afternoon."

"No, let's not talk about it anymore. I shouldn't have said
anything at all."

"Marcia, that's not true. You were perfectly right to share,
that's what the group is for. It just happens that some of our
members are more interested in talking than in listening. But I
was listening, and I heard you say that God wasn't hearing your
prayers."

"Not that he doesn't hear, exactly, but that I don't feel like he
hears. We're supposed to thank God and praise him for everything, but I don't feel thankful at all. I just feel tired."

She looked around the room in despair; toys were scattered
across the rug, newspapers and magazines lay in heaps beneath
end tables. Marcia sank into a chair and clutched her head in her
hands, hot tears dripping between her fingers. "What's wrong

with me, Sophie, what's wrong with me?" She picked up a crushed box of tissues that lay on the back of the couch. "All Jack has to do lately is look at me and I start crying." She shook her head and made a weak effort to laugh at herself, then sighed. "Sophie, what do you do when you get so tired that you just want to forget everything and run away?"

"I sit."

Marcia looked up from the shredded tissue. "You sit?"

"I sit and do nothing for about ten or fifteen minutes. Meditation. I usually focus my attention on the Lord, but it isn't like I'm praying or anything. I just sit and relax all over, and I don't really *think* of anything at all. After a while, I feel better than when I've had a good night's sleep."

Later Sophie brought over some books on meditation for Marcia to study. One was specifically for Christians, and talked a lot about the Bible and saints. The others were not particularly religious, and advocated meditation simply as a form of relaxation. All one had to do was sit still and do nothing. Since Marcia had always thought she could not do anything right, she reckoned she should be able to do nothing very well.

At first the exercises had been unbearably boring. Then there was the problem of finding a quiet location. But gradually, as the summer wore away, she found herself looking forward to her meditations, alert for a few minutes when she could slip away and merely be still; to sit quietly, feet flat on the floor, hands in her lap, eyes closed. Usually the sound of water focused her attention, whether it was from the tub, from the children playing in the hose outside, or from the laundry in the basement. Eventually the water noises shaped themselves into impressions of greater forms, of rivers and streams, waterfalls and torrents, and the thoughts of the world around her were forgotten. It was on the river that she had first seen Ceyx.

Sophie had told her when she began that it was wise to have a guide, a spiritual advisor to encourage and help her as she began to explore the depths of her own spirit, and from the beginning it was natural for the elder to guide the novice. "The world of the spirit is uncharted territory, you know," Sophie warned. "And even though meditation is older than Christianity, every person is a pioneer. Try always to focus on a Scriptural image, and never sit longer than twenty minutes at a time."

Marcia had problems with her focus. Although Sophie suggested that she concentrate on Jesus, it was not that easy. Weighty titles crowded against her mind: king, judge, lord and master, everlasting father . . . unknowingly, her image of the Son of God was compiled of all the authoritarian experiences of her past; a critical father, the shouted sermons of a thousand zealous preachers, lightning bolts and judges in heavy black robes. Mingled with these were the hidden thoughts—the impossible, unthinkable disappointments of her marriage, the love that hurt, tenderness that demanded servitude, the eternal authority—leading, ruling, crushing, hurting, all by the sanction of love. No, there was no rest for her in the name of Jesus. Somebody else might be good, strong, and wise. Someone like an angel.

She had first seen him in midsummer, while Josh and Davy were drowning each other outside with the hose. She had pulled a chair close to a window so she could hear if they called, and closed her eyes. The sound of water filled her mind until it overflowed into a river that flooded out across the distant plains of herself. Far away the light of life shone golden across the water and reached toward her. The river surged out of the sunlight, and she was rushing, soaring into that life. In the infinite distance, out of the light itself flashed a streak of lightning, glowing above the sun like the morning star. Closer it came, a bolt of pure power, then gradually it took the form of a great bird, wheeling and dipping, exhibiting the grace and majesty of pefect flight. After a very long while, the figure swooped suddenly down upon her. Beneath the arching wings of glory was not the form of a bird, but the shape of a man, a god. In wonder and terror Marcia hung helpless. Bright gladness shone from his face, and the awesome body glowed as though burning within. His hands were lifted in welcome, and the fire in his eyes was darker than the depths of hell.

"I am Ceyx. I am your guide."

Marcia's head snapped back. Visions dissolved in puddles and splinters of light, and she saw her husband glaring over her, holding their two-year-old in his arms. The child's face was smeared with tears and dirt, and his knee was bloody. "What do you think you are doing? Look at Davy! He was pulling at the door, crying and screaming, and you won't even let him into the house!"

She struggled to bring her thoughts together, "What is it? Why are you here?"

"Why am I here?" Jack's voice was approaching the danger level. "It's six o'clock, that's why I'm here! And I come home to find my son bleeding, and his mother spaced out in some damned trance! And you ask why I'm here?"

Taking Davy gently from his father, she steered him toward the bathroom. Her mind was clearing and, rather than feeling upset, she was calm and faintly amused. "Be quiet, Jack, you're scaring the boy. You're making too much fuss over a little scratch." Davy quieted as Mommy washed his face with kisses and smoothed a bandage on the scraped knee. The glow of light on golden waters still warmed her, and she felt lifted on the balance of those powerful wings. Marcia did not realize that for the first time in their marriage she had told Jack to be quiet. But she did know that she had lost all awareness for more than three hours, and the situation might have been much worse.

Now while Marcia was remembering these things, making the beds, Sophie called to see if she needed a ride to the prayer group that afternoon.

"Did you find the books I told you about at the library?"

"Yes, last week, sorry I haven't gotten back to you sooner," Marcia answered. "As a matter of fact, I should tell you what happened. I made the mistake of taking the boys along, and Davy threw one of his screaming tantrums. So I got him to quit crying and was heading out the door when guess who was coming in . . . Helen Gussets!"

"Oh, Marcia."

"And she had to make a remark as to what fine boys I had and how they just witnessed to the world what a good mother I was; and of course it was obvious what she really meant."

"Now be fair, Marcia. Perhaps she just thought you needed cheering up."

"I doubt it, not Helen. But then she had to examine a novel I had checked out . . . you know, a romantic fiction. Well, of course she opened it up and saw a four-letter word, then started preaching about how we need to fill our minds with truth and beauty, and she handed me a copy of some dumb periodical for the 'Christian Homemaker.' She said I ought to use my leisure time to some 'edifying purpose."

"Marcia, Helen doesn't mean any harm."

"The thing that really gripes me is that the word she found so unedifying was nothing but the basic Anglo-Saxon word for the crap I clean out of the house all day. What does pure-minded, clean-hands Helen Gussets know of diapers and cat litter and wet sheets and piles behind the furniture? The 'Christian Home-maker' can mop it up, but she can't say it, not even if her mouth is full of it!"

"Marcia, I hope you didn't blow up at Helen."

"Who me? Never. But she examined the other books, and I told her that you and I were doing studies in experimental prayer and that we planned to revive the church through fasting and meditation."

"You didn't!"

"And she was greatly impressed and asked me to tell her all about it. So I gave her that book on meditation and weight control."

"You're totally depraved," Sophie cried in mock exasperation. "I hope you came home and begged forgiveness on your knees."

"Nope. I came home, spanked the boys and put them to bed, then sat down and meditated for an hour and a half."

"Wait a minute. Back up. You meditated for an hour and a half? Ninety minutes? Honey, no one meditates for more than fifteen or twenty minutes. Not even the medieval monks did more than that . . . except the crazy ones who ran off into caves and ate bats and became saints. You aren't wearing a hair shirt, are you?"

"Sorry to disappoint you, but a cave doesn't sound like a bad idea. No interruptions."

"How do you meditate for an hour and a half, anyway, with those two wild things underfoot? Not to mention Jack . . . ."

"I overcame that. I wait until they are all asleep, then I can sit without being bothered as long as I please."

"How long is as long as you please?" Sophie asked.

"Usually an hour and a half . . . sometimes longer." Marcia hesitated, but Sophie waited expectantly, so she finally said, "Sometimes three hours."

"Three hours, and after Jack is asleep—Marcia, when do you sleep?"

"I get enough rest, I really do. I don't seem to need as much sleep since I've learned to meditate, and I don't get tired, either. And the house is clean, the beds are made, not a dish in the sink. Sophie, I've never felt better!"

They drove together to the meeting that afternoon, and Marcia thought that the group was greatly entertaining. Helen had to tell everyone how she had begun to meditate in the past week. "And it is just the most wonderful thing!" she gushed. "When I am in the spirit, I just feel totally free. Sophie, you simply must share with everyone what this new form of prayer is that we have discovered."

"Oh, Helen, there is nothing new about meditation," Sophie objected, but she complied and explained the practice as simply as she could. Dorothy Classon decided that it was her place to offer a mature opinion. "Meditation is certainly a wholesome discipline for Christians to undertake. But as women, we must not go off on these spiritual experiments on our own. It was the woman, you know, who was originally deceived. It is essential that each of your husbands, or whoever is your spiritual authority, is fully aware of your intention. And you must certainly report any impression, or spiritual word that you receive, to your pastor for his discernment."

Marcia listened in silence, holding her hand before her face to conceal a little smile she could not restrain. The notion of telling Jack what she had seen in the spiritual realm was too ridiculous. Dear as he was, he could not understand what happened to her there any more than he could understand how it felt to have a baby. And to imagine telling Pastor Classon about Ceyx . . . the thought was too much and she almost choked. Helen noticed. "Just look at Marcia. You can see what the practice of meditation has done for her. She's not the melancholy little thing she used to be; she is fairly bursting with joy!"

Later, after the coffee cups and books were cleared away and they started for home, Marcia found her friend unusually silent.

"Sophie, what's the matter? Have I said something wrong?"

"No, I'm sorry, you haven't done anything wrong. It's just that I am awfully worried about you, about what you may have gotten into."

"You mean my meditations are too long."

"Yes, but I'm wondering if you are meditating at all. Wait, listen. When people meditate, they don't become oblivious to everything around them. They don't go off into another world. I can focus on the Lord, and experience his presence, but at the same time I can look at the clock, or hear the phone ring. I don't become hypnotized."

"Sophie, I'm not hypnotized. And I don't go into a trance."

"Maybe those are the wrong terms. But there is something more. You told me that the angel who is your guide is named Ceyx, right? C-E-Y-X?"

"Honestly, Sophie, I don't know how to spell it. What does it matter?"

"Marcia, I looked up that name and it is not in the Bible. But it is in Greek mythology. Ceyx was a king, married to a woman named Alcyone, and they were both turned into birds when they died. Ceyx was a son of Lucifer."

Sophie stopped for a red light, and the two women looked at one another. "What do you mean, a son of Lucifer? I thought the devil in mythology was Pluto or somebody."

"He is, but Lucifer is also in the Greek myths, and he is called the light-bearer, or the morning star. The devil is called Lucifer in Isaiah, and that also means the morning star."

"That doesn't mean that my angel . . . he can't be, you've never seen him, or you couldn't imagine such a thing."

"But, dearest, that is just the point. You have seen him, so you can't imagine it. And think about the light. When you first saw him, didn't you say that you were going up the river, into the light—you called it the light of life—and now you are going down the river, away from the light? Marcia, the images are all wrong."

"Sophie, stop, you're scaring me. What do you want me to do? I can't just walk up to an angel and ask him if he is a son of Lucifer."

"No, don't do that. But ask him about Jesus. Ask him about the cross, and the resurrection and the blood of the Lamb. And ask him where you are going; where you are headed down the river."

"All right. I'll try, but I don't know if I can. When I am with him, I don't think about anything else. When I am at the river, I forget about everything except what I see in the spirit. But I will try."

It was some time after midnight when Marcia came downstairs alone to begin her meditations. She set a candle on the dining room table, and warmed the leftover coffee, absent-mindedly rubbing a new bruise on her shoulder. Jack was not actually rough, she told herself, just over-enthusiastic. It takes a great lover to produce a girl, he said, and he had made his best effort.

She closed her eyes. Feet together, hands loosely clasped in her lap, breathe deeply, in, out. Glare from the lamp overhead made orange patterns on her eyelids. Light. Concentrate on the light.

Moving, turning light, great rivers of light falling down from above her, across her face, over her skin, into her hands, bounding against her feet. She turned slightly and saw that she was sitting among flowering shrubs whose heavy clusters of pale pink blossoms waved a tingling fragrance of spices through the air. She rose, picked a cluster for her hair, then began to walk down the slope along the river, brushing aside the drooping branches and unbelievably soft grasses as she passed. Her feet were bare.

The Angel was sitting on a rock in the midst of the stream. The shining water swirled around him, and Marcia could see the reflections of his wings like diamonds in the waves. "Come to me."

Though the river was clear as glass, she could see no bottom. "How shall I come? Is it deep?"

"Come on the water."

Of course. She set her foot cautiously onto the river, and it broke the surface just as it would in the physical world, wet and almost icy cold. She lifted her foot and tried again, this time concentrating on keeping her foot on the water. It worked. She could feel the firm but soft surface sliding under the sole of her foot; wet, yet solid and moving like a conveyor belt come alive.

Stepping from the bank, she found each foot moving separately along the rush of the current. Another moment and she would have lost her balance completely, but the Angel caught her hand and she was on the rock beside him.

"Walking on water is easier on a still pond. But here, where water is alive, still ponds are difficult to find."

It was hard to think about what he was saying, because the Angel still held her hand. His touch was gentle, but it burned like fire, fire like the fire in brandy, burning and sweet. It was the first time he had touched her, and she didn't want to let go.

"You have come with questions today."

Struggling to think while the sweet fire was searing through her palm, Marcia stammered, "Sophie asked me so many things . . . about Scripture. And about . . . about . . . ." The fire devoured her hand and she could no longer speak.

"About the Christ. Yes, Sophie would ask such things. And she is correct, of course, for herself. She is immature in spiritual things, and finds great comfort in old images. You are beyond that."

The liquid fire surged upward through Marcia's wrist into her arm. Sophie is immature; I am beyond that.

"Of course the Christ is here. But you shall know what Sophie can never understand, and that is in this world we no longer bear our earthly titles. Scripture teaches you to live by the spirit, not by the letter of the Law. Here the Scripture itself, which is the Law, has passed away."

Fire was in her chest now, rushing across her back. The light of the river became scarlet flames as the fire surged into her face; her very hair seemed to bristle with heat. The voice of the Angel rode on the flames through her mind, and his voice became the fire within and without.

"When the new has come, the old shall pass away. This fleshly body shall put on a new, glorious body. The one who comes shall be baptised with fire. The spirit is a consuming fire."

The words "consuming fire" fell like a sheet of flame across her breasts, through her belly, bursting from her loins like a fiery child leaping from her womb. She fell, burning, into the river of flames. Her head hit the floor as she fell, and the cup of coffee spilled onto the carpet.

Washing the dishes by the kitchen window the next morning, Marcia poured water through the morning sunlight, trying to re-create the colors that had danced on the shining river. Running the children's bath, she pressed her hand against the water, feeling for that liquid firmness that had supported her feet in the spirit realm. But more than the light, more than the water or even walking on the water, Marcia thought of the fire. Nothing before in her life had felt so intensely physical as that burning; no pain, no pleasure, not even her deepest intimacy with Jack had been so intense. Marcia smiled ruefully to herself. Certainly not her intimacy with Jack. Painful, yes, but not intense, and never intense with sweetness that made the pain ecstatic. She thought of the hand of the Angel; it certainly had felt like a physical hand, muscular, strong, steady, lifting her from the river to the rock. Thinking of his hand made her own hands tremble.

Jack began to be afraid for his wife when he sat at dinner that evening. The potatoes were scorched, and the meat dry and tasteless. How could she explain that she had forgotten what she was doing while watching the little blue flames rise around the skillet?

"He just doesn't understand how I could burn myself with a candle," Marcia said as she and Sophie were folding clothes several days later. Marcia had become sick with a fever, so the children had been sent to their grandmother's again, and Sophie was giving a hand with the day's chores. Sophie's hands moved swiftly through the piles of towels, sorting, folding, arranging in neat stacks. With the tape and gauze around her thumb and two fingers, Marcia was slow and clumsy, and finally sat fidgeting with a washcloth.

"How did you burn yourself like that? I guess I'm as puzzled as Jack."

"I don't know. I set the thing on the table when I began meditating. It was in a holder." Her words were slow. "Then when I came to myself, the wax was all over my hand, and it hurt, and wouldn't come off, so I woke up Jack and he got me cleaned up and bandaged. He didn't yell at me—I almost wish he had. He just kept looking at me and he must have said ten times how worried he was. I think he thinks I'm going nuts."

"No, he doesn't. He just doesn't understand, and he *is* worried about you." Sophie set the folded clothes into a basket and opened the refrigerator to find some juice. "It's time for your aspirin again." When she brought the drink and medicine she felt Marcia's forehead. "I think your temperature is going up, my dear. Does your head hurt?"

Marcia stared blankly for a moment. "No, I don't think so."

"How about your stomach? Or your neck, does it hurt when I rub it?"

"No, nothing hurts. It's just so hot, and I can't breathe. Can we open some windows or something?"

"We've got the air conditioner on full blast. There's just humidity outside anyway. Why don't you go upstairs to bed, and let me finish down here? You need to get some sleep."

"No, I don't want to sleep, I want to talk." Her actions contradicted her words. She could barely hold her head up and her hands dropped heavily on the table.

"All right, what shall we talk about?" Sophie sat down and offered a cold washcloth to wipe her face. "Pick a subject."

Marcia stared vacantly at the window, and murmured, "So hot outside." Her hands clenched, pulling at the gauze. "What do you think it is like to die?"

"To die?" Sophie thought a few moments. "I think that death is a continuation of whatever state the dying one is in at the point of death. Not a continuation, exactly, but a heightening, a magnification. I don't mean the physical state . . . oh, dear, what do I mean? You've caught me off guard, and my theology is a little stale." She carried the laundry out of the room while she groped for words. "I am trying to say that I believe we exist to a great extent in eternity right now, and that death merely heightens our awareness of that eternal state."

"You don't think that death is an escape, and end to suffering?"

"Death isn't an end, any more than birth is an end. No, anyone trying to escape into death will find themselves in the arms of whatever they were trying to escape from."

Marcia's face went white, and Sophie realized that she had said the wrong thing. "Marcia, what is it? Oh, honey, you're crying, here, sit up, let me see your face. Here, come on."

"No, it's all right, I'm all right." Her voice was barely audible, and she trembled pitifully. "I really don't know why I'm crying. It's just the children, what will they do? I shouldn't leave Jack, but he's strong and he can manage, but I do feel bad about the children." Sophie grasped her hands to try to still their frantic clenching and clawing at the bandage. The fingers were icy cold, while her forehead was burning with fever. "I wouldn't do it, but I know that's what he wants, and it must be right. Jack says I'm a good girl, and I want to be good, Jack, but it is so hard to leave."

"Why are you leaving, Marcia?"

"I . . . I'm not sure, I don't know. It must be the fire, it's so hot and I can't think and I can't remember." She dropped her head, sobbing weakly.

"You're absolutely right, it is the fire, and it's the fever, and it's no wonder you cannot remember anything. Do you think it will be any cooler upstairs? Let's see if you can step into a cool bath, and it might take care of some of that fire." Sophie took her by the arm and Marcia allowed herself to be guided. The stairs were difficult; Sophie was a small woman and Marcia was weaker by the moment, but the effort kept her fevered thoughts away from death and fire. In the bathroom, though, the sight of water stirred up images and she began to murmur about living waters and other things that Sophie had difficulty following. But as she stepped into the ordinary tub waters, they had the desired effect of somewhat relieving the fever.

"Sophie, I've been talking a little crazy, haven't I?"

"Oh, not really crazy. Just about fire and water, and crystal streams that fall from the sky and dance like lightning over burning lilies. That's lovely, you know. Lean forward, and I'll rub your back."

"They weren't lilies, exactly, they were more like daffodils, with a crown in the center, and petals opening out all around. Not on fire, but made of fire, and hanging in great garlands from the willow trees. And when we walked underneath, it smelled like burning incense, and I was afraid my hair would be scorched."

"Can you stand up? I'll get you a towel, here. Tell me more; was this your vision last night?"

"No, this was several night—oh, I'm dizzy. No, that was several nights ago. We left the river and went into the forest. It's cool and dark under the willows. But I know that we're coming back to the river again, because I can hear it somewhere close by."

"You're with Ceyx?"

"I'm always with Ceyx. He never leaves me."

"Don't sit down here, let's go into the bedroom. Not too fast now." Marcia sat on the end of the bed, and Sophie looked for a robe.

"I don't want to rest, I want to talk. You're the only one who doesn't think I'm nuts. I can't tell anybody else."

"Okay, you are in the forest. I'm listening. Is it as beautiful there as beside the river?"

"No. It's dark and misty, like the sun has just gone down, or is ready to come up. I don't know which, but there is not much light, and it is hard to make things out. And there are animals. That seems strange because all along the river we only saw a few butterflies, and sometimes a bird way up in the clouds. But last night, and all the while we have been in the woods, there have been animals all around. There was a leopard first. It seemed so friendly, like our tabby. But it never let me get close enough to touch it. And after the leopard came the lion, and that was really wild, I mean, it wasn't playing or anything. It looked like it was starved, and it ripped up the ground with its claws, and it kept circling as we walked. Then the last thing was a wolf. I just heard it growling and whining through the underbrush, all thin and bony. It may have been a dog, but I felt like it was a wolf."

"Oh, and the bird. There was this large bird that I could barely see through the tops of the trees. It was very large, and brown or gold. When the trees were too thick to see it, I could tell it was still there because it would give these little cries, like it was calling for something."

Sophie wrapped a light blanket over Marcia's legs. "Maybe it was another angel, like Ceyx."

"No, this was a bird. You can tell the difference once you see them. This bird had big wings, but they were clearly feathers; I could see that, even though it was so far away. Ceyx's wings are different; they are like light, like all colors whirling together in those beautiful white wings. And they're made of the finest gossamer, like spiderwebs and silk, and full of power. The bird was nothing like that. Their voices are different, too. The bird's cry was just a big bird crying, but Ceyx's voice is a spirit; you don't hear it with your ears exactly. You feel it inside you, and it is full of music, and—and magic."

"You sound like a teenager talking about her new boyfriend."

"I know, I'm sorry. But everything seems better if I can explain it to you."

"What seems better?"

"Staying. He told me before that I could stay if I wanted to, but I never really thought about it. But now he says that we can't go any further unless I make the decision to stay. And I think that I have decided. I know if you put your hand to the plow and look back you are not worthy of the Kingdom, so I try not to look back. But I shouldn't leave Jack and the—and the children. Then I think of the verse that says whoever gives up children and home and riches and things will receive so much more. And if I refuse, I'll be cast into the outer darkness, and then there is the fire, and I feel so hot, Sophie, I'm so hot, what can I do? Jack, where's Jack? Help me, I'm so confused." Her hands were tearing at the bandage again, and sweat popped out on her forehead.

"Hush, it's all right, you don't have to do anything. It's all right. Drink this juice, that's right. We'll leave the glass right here on the table beside you. Here, try to lie down. Hush now, it's just the fever, it makes everything seem confused."

"But I have to decide."

"Yes, but not right now. You are sick, and you cannot do anything right now."

"But Ceyx . . . ."

"Ceyx can wait until you are well. That's better, relax. Now, I want to suggest something so that you can get some rest. Do not meditate again tonight. Don't meditate or even pray for several days until you are completely well. Let me pray for you. You are exhausted and you need to rest, doctor's orders. If you start thinking about Ceyx, or about the children, or any of those things, I want you just to tell yourself, 'Sophie is taking care of that,' or 'That's Sophie's problem.' I'm going to concentrate on Ceyx for you, and on your children, and when you are well, we'll talk it all out, okay? You just rest, and let me carry the burden for awhile."

That afternoon and later at her own home, Sophie carried out her promise. Sitting quietly she imagined Marcia, carefully re-creating in her mind every characteristic of her friend: her appearance, her movements, her manner of speaking and gestures. She tired to imagine her wandering, frightened, through a misty forest. Then Sophie meditated on the angel, building up an image from the descriptions she had: iridescent wings, glowing face, powerful muscles, looming over Marcia, seductive and deadly. Then she imagined them separate, the angel drifting further and further away, shrinking, fading from view, and Marcia turning, smiling, becoming stronger. The process took only a few minutes, but she concentrated on it with all intention and faith, and repeated the exercise several times through the day. She also called Helen Gussets.

If there was any gift with which Mrs. Gussets was liberally endowed, it was a talent for minding other people's business. When she learned that Marcia was ill, she responded with concern and sympathy that bordered closely on delight. "Why, no, Marcia's mother can't take care of those boys for another day, why, her arthritis is very bad. Sara Miller ought to be watching those children, and I know that she would be more than glad to take them. And we'll have to organize about meals, at least for the rest of the week. Let's see, lunches are all right, but we'll have to make sure there is something in the house for breakfast, so that means someone will need to do some shopping. And there will be laundry to do, and, Sophie, what did the house look like, will there be cleaning to do? . . . you did! Well, aren't you a wonder, I must say, you have done more than your part. I'll just call some of the other girls, and we'll get these little things taken care of. I've got to run, so much to do! Thank you for calling me, dear!"

By morning the girls were sufficiently organized so that coffee-cake and donuts arrived for breakfast, along with a committee of house cleaners. Marcia's doctor prescribed antibiotics and a mild sedative, and the fever was gradually coming down. Sophie had little to do but to continue support in prayer. All seemed to be going well until she telephoned on the third evening, and Mrs. Gussets answered.

"Helen, where is Jack? Is everything all right?"

"Oh, my dear, of course you don't know. They just left for the hospital. It's been two hours now."

"The hospital? Is the fever worse? Helen, tell me what's going on."

"Yes, worse, much worse, they say she is in a coma now and when Jack found her they said that she wasn't breathing and there may be brain damage. And they found that her heart wasn't working properly, either, so they just took her right away to the intensive care room. Doctors can do wonderful things, but you and I know that when the Lord calls, you have to go, and there's nothing that doctors or medicine can do to change that. She was just too good for this world, you could see it in her eyes as she lay there, her heart was in heaven already. But it's those little boys I feel for. I just put them to bed, all asking for their mommy, and I had to tell them that she was so sick, and might not come home. Oh, that little Joshua, he's such a little man, just like his daddy. But Davy, oh, how he cried, and you have to expect it, he's just a baby. My heart was breaking to hear them say their sweet little prayers, and knowing she's not coming home again. Now I'm crying again. I know that it is God's will, but it is hard. And poor Jack, just about out of his mind, you know how he worshipped her. I have always thought of them as the perfect couple, you know, him so loving and all. And now this, well, God's will is hard."

"Helen, you said that Jack found her . . . what do you mean?

I thought he was staying home with her while the fever was high."

"Oh, Sophie, the fever broke. Yes, the fever broke sometime last night. This morning she was up and feeling so much better, and insisted that Jack go to work. Sara offered to take the boys again, so Jack thought she would be all right on her own, and could have a nice quiet day. He's always that thoughtful and concerned for her, you know. I would have been more than glad to come over, and just let my own housework hang. There isn't a whole lot to do when you live by yourself, but there is the dust, you know, and things do pile up, but I would have come and stayed. But she insisted that she wanted to rest and be alone, to spend some time in prayer, she said. So of course I didn't want to intrude. But when Jack came home, and he came home early which is probably the only thing that saved her, there she was, sitting on the edge of the bed, just blazing with fever. I understand that she was choking, or gasping for air, or not breathing at all. When the ambulance came they put oxygen on and took her to intensive care right away. Then he called me, and I picked up the children at Sara's and fed them and put them to bed. I'll just stay here as long as I'm needed. God gives us all burdens to bear, and if this is mine, I'll just do the best I can."

"Helen, which hospital is she in?"

"Oh, General. In intensive care."

"I have to go, Helen, thank you. You are a blessing. Goodbye."

Sophie hurried to the car and drove toward the downtown hospital. Helen was excitable, but if Marcia had in fact been taken to intensive care, the situation could hardly be exaggerated. Sophie had no doubt that the fever which was so out of control was of spiritual origin.

Why had she not seen Marcia's weakness? Was it pride in her mystic maturity that caused her to proselytize a friend, or had she really offered honest aid to a desperate need? She had loosened Marcia's bondage to Jack's insensitivity only to find her snared by another spirit of bondage. If she could find her, and with God's help deliver her now, she would lead her gently (as she should have in the beginning) toward the light of Christian freedom Marcia had never known. Sophie felt the weight of sin and prayed for pardon as she worked through the city traffic.

If she had led Marcia into the wilderness, then she might be able to lead her out; if she could descend like Orpheus to find the one that was lost . . . only Marcia was not yet lost, she was still alive. Then she would not need to descend through the gates of hell, but only to the courtyard, to the wood between the worlds where Virgil had found Dante. Sophie searched her memory for another precendent, but her thoughts eluded her and she turned into the visitor's parking lot. It was nearly deserted and she wondered vaguely whether she would be admitted to the ICU as she walked through the automatic doors into the hospital.

Sophie tried to step quietly over the clattering tiles as she passed each bed in the ward where hope was reduced to pinpoints of green and red light flickering against black monitor screens. If Jack had not been beside the bed, she might not have recognized Marcia at all. Her friend's head was wrapped in a wet towel; ice-packs melted at her neck and under her arms. The skin about her face was as taut and transparent as alabaster; breath came in feeble pants between cracked lips, and the eyes stared vaguely with un-natural brightness.

"Jack, I hope I'm not intruding. I wanted to see her so much." Sophie laid her hand on Jack's shoulder and he gave a slight nod. She found a vinyl chair across the aisle and drew it close to Marcia's head, then took one of the unresponsive hands in her own. She looked around, afraid that one of the staff might inter-fere, wondering how to begin what she was determined to do. Leaning closer to the bed she tried to speak softly. She hesitated, uncertain of her direction, then said with determination, "Marcia, I'm coming to bring you home."

She bent still closer, leaning her forehead over the perspiring form. The last vision had been of the dark forest, full of the move-ment of animals and falling water. She set her imagination upon that forest: great trees with tangled branches huddling in the gloom, mist rising from brackish pools hidden beneath moulder-ing leaves and creeping moss. Knotted roots and knees uprooted the path, constantly turning the wanderer aside, pulling one deeper, closer into the cold heart of the dying forest. Sophie concentrated on the image until she shivered with a damp chill. Then she focused on the animals.

First the playful leopard, seeming so harmless as it gamboled first at a distance, then closer, to the left of the path and now on the right, circling, drawing ever nearer. Sophie held the image of the leopard for a moment, then went on. She must find the lion next. Pride and power took shape in her mind and formed them-selves into the physical expression of their eternal essence. Nearly hidden within the trees, prowling, watching, approaching and cutting off her path until it was close enough for her to see the flecks of gold shaken from the heavy mane, head thrown back, body quivering, clawing at the ground. She refused to move until she felt she must scream from fear, then she let the vision go.

Her buttocks were growing stiff on the rigid seat. She could hear the faint click and hum of the monitors, and even lift her head to acknowledge a nurse passing the evening rounds. She set herself totally within another realm, yet was not lost to her own.

The wolf was last, and as Marcia had not directly encountered this beast, Sophie did not attempt to develop its impression. She heard a creeping within the undergrowth, a menacing growl, a gaunt shadow among other shadows, and that was all.

Now she made herself listen until she could hear the sound of the river, flowing thick and slow through the wild wast of the valley. When the direction was clear she turned her steps down-ward, letting the ground beneath her feet become soggy and suck up into her sandals. The river itself, its flow clogged with rotting weeds, was barely distinguishable from the mud beside it.

As she looked upstream, a patch of grey sky showed among the branches that overhung the river. The path downstream was more open, and as she turned to follow it she found the oozing mud pulled less at her steps. Gradually the banks of damp clay rose higher beside her, and a mild breeze encouraged her from behind. As she went on, the way appeared lighter, and she turned for a moment to see if the sun might indeed be rising. Immediately her feet began to slip on the bank, and when she tried to retrace a few steps found the slope so steep and slimy that any effort to return was all but impossible. Only the way down was fast and firm. And still the river moved beside her, reluctant and slow.

A growing chill began to creep up her spine, partly from the damp wind that pushed her on, but more from revulsion to the path itself, and to its sure destination. The clay bank had risen beside her on the right until it now loomed over her head, offering no root to grip or stone to give foothold for escape. It seemed that the road would continue forever, moving always effortlessly downward without alternative, without end. Then abruptly, it did end.

The bank fell suddenly away and the river curved in a wide sweep to the south. Before her stretched a vast rocky plain, barren of life, strewn with broken stone and rubble. How far it extended to the south or north she could not tell, for the shadow of the forest fell heavy as a shroud over the naked ground. The path no longer followed the river but ran straight on across the rocks. Sophie did not follow it. Directly before her, rising from the debris and engulfing the path, rose a tower of flame.

She stood frozen, gazing into that flame. It neither withdrew nor advanced but burned steadily, a perfect column of fire. It threw out scorching heat but, though visible itself, it gave no light, and behind it fell a deep shadow obliterating any view of what might lie beyond. The fire was immense, perhaps twenty feet or more across, if conventional forms of measurement had any meaning in this world between the worlds. It was terrifying, but also beautiful. Tongues of flame wove patterns of blue and green above embers of scarlet and gold, magnetic and hypnotizing like a cozy hearth on an autumn night, or a camper's bonfire at the end of a long trail. It danced, it beckoned. It sang, and its song was like the roar of a bottomless waterfall. Sophie felt herself moving irrationally toward it, reacting like a moth to a candle.

"Excuse me, ma'am, visitors are not allowed in the ward at this time," The nurse touched her on the arm and Sophie realized that she must appear to have fallen asleep at the bedside. "Oh, I can't leave now, I've just started . . . ." She groped weakly for an explanation. "I need to go on . . . to pray for her."

The nurse studied the chart and set a fresh IV on the stand, carefully adjusting the flow. She glanced a moment at the monitors, then studied Sophie again. Her mouth was set in a grim line. "Are you family? Members of the immediate family are permitted to stay with a critical patient at all times."

"Let her stay. She's a sister." It was Jack. Sophie shot him a look of gratitude but he returned to his silent vigil. His face was grey, drawn with shadows of weariness and despair. She wondered how many nights he had wakened alone while Marcia meditated, and at the pain he must feel watching his wife drawn away by a power he could neither fight nor understand. The nurse nodded and passed on to the next bed.

Sophie bent her head to gaze into the fire again, but now with horror and understanding. This was the force that had lured Marcia to destruction; here was the fever that at this moment consumed her life. She studied the fire, trying to see if there was any form or shadow within it that might be a woman, or what a woman may have become once submitted to that burning embrace. There was no sign, no alteration as it rose far above the rock. As she was looking into the flaming heights, a bird appeared high above and wheeled out of view, then materialized again through the smoking clouds. A winged creature, not angelic in form but in essence, an eagle with gleaming talons and fearful beak. It swooped and vanished behind the fire and appeared again. Sophie suddenly knew that this image was no more a construction of her imagination than was the tower of flame; these figures were vivid with an existence of their own, and she was conscious of her weakness in the realm of these powers.

The shadow passed overhead once more. Irrationally she remembered a childhood experience of flying in a glider. The fragile craft had been lifted above the runway by a small plane, then released to soar effortlessly over the fields, catching the air currents to rise, circling higher and riding the winds. The memory became more vivid, and she seemed to be riding those winds again, looking down on green trees and fields, over a dark forest and purple rivers. Then she broke through a thick cloud of smoke and saw the black stream far below, and the rising column of fire. A great sense of peace, of balance and poise sustained her, and she moved at that height with no sensation of fear. Closer she, or they, came to the fire, and with the eyes of the eagle she could see tiny and half concealed, like a mouse beneath a thistle, the form of a woman within the flames.

"Marcia." The voice that called was her own, yet it was not she who spoke, "Marcia, turn around." No response came from below, but a great sensation of weakness rose with the clouds of smoke, and wave after wave of black despair. "Marcia, turn around." Again the sense of helplessness came to her, and what might have been a voice, faint as thought, "I can't." The third time Sophie's voice called, reaching with all the strength of eternity, "Marcia, turn." Then at last there was movement, or perhaps only the intention of movement, a minute variation of shadow within the darkness of the flame. Or it may have been only a quickening of pulse in the fevered palm which lay in Sophie's hand on the bed. It was enough, and the eagle plunged.

Straight into the column of fire it hurled itself, like a phoenix into its nest through the scorched air into the heart of the flames, and Sophie fell with it, seared by the blasting wind. She felt the blaze expand in her brain, then all was darkness and she gave herself up to death.

A moment or a century passed, and she woke prostrate on a rock. Above her rose the angelic being Marcia had described from her meditation: glistening bronze flesh, gossamer wings, and a face so full of gladness that it glowed with the brightness of the sun. Whether the fire had been quenched by the eagle's plunge, or whether she simply saw the angel now with Marcia's eyes she did not know, but the only flames were those that now burned darkly in his eyes. The monster held Marcia in his embrace. Her arms were locked to her sides, her face buried against the glowing expanse of his breast. Sophie wanted to slide off the rock, to run, to scream for the eagle to snatch her away. If Ceyx moved his foot he could crush her like a paper cup. Or worse, if he chose to take her up into that burning embrace, how could she resist? She lay as she had fallen, afraid to move for many heartbeats. Then he saw her and smiled.

"Now you have come. Come, my precious, into my joy." Promises of pleasure and delight, forbidden ecstasies and un-dreamt-of sensualities, opened to her in that smile. Fragrances of islands and perfumed waters, music from beyond the heavens, awakened in her soul. He reached out a hand and it dripped with pungent oils. Then a winged shadow fell between them as the distant cry of the eagle broke like cold water on her mind. Ceyx's hand was still stretched out toward her and in the gesture he had partly released Marcia. Without thought, Sophie leaped forward and seized Marcia's arm where it hung limp at the creature's side, and jerked with all her strength. To her complete amazement there was no resistance and the two fell clear. Immediately came a roar and a blast that tore at their clothes and knocked them off their feet. The rock shook, and the river waters behind them foamed and crashed as though trying to escape the terrible fury that rose in towering flames. No seductive cozy fire now, but a raging inferno that breathed the hateful sulfur of hell.

Marcia clutched at her friend where they lay, wailing in terror, burying her face in her arms. But Sophie looked straight into the fire and felt no more fear. She knew now as the eagle had known, that this demon had no power but seduction. It could not reach them with the flames; it could terrify but never touch. "Look at it now, look, Marcia. This is Ceyx. You must see him as he is." Marcia obeyed, reluctantly, then gradually with recognition and disgust. Tears ran over her cheeks and her hands trembled as she clung to Sophie's arm. "Oh, dear Lord, what can I do? Sophie, what have I done?"

Sophie folded the trembling hands in her own. "It's all right now, it's all finished." This soul was as fragile and close to death as the body lying beneath the monitors in the hospital bed. "I'll help you. Just turn around and we'll go back toward the light."

"To Jack?"

"Well, we'll bring Jack along, if he will come."

Together they rose from the rock with their backs against the dark blaze. They faced the mountain far away, and above them the wings of the eagle shone golden in the light of the rising sun.

Sophie looked up. A nurse was removing the ice packs from around Marcia's face and arms. Jack was standing across the bed and mistook the wonder in her eyes for alarm. "It's all right, she's asleep. The fever broke about half an hour ago, and the nurse says she's sleeping normally." He brushed a damp curl from his wife's forehead and she stirred slightly, as any sleeper might stir at the lover's caress. "She's sweating a lot, but feel how cool her skin is."

Reaching for a final touch to Marcia's cheek, Sophie turned to leave, then Jack stopped her. "Listen, thanks for being here. I don't know why, but it helped to have someone to bear the burden with me."

She smiled, realizing how tired she was. "I'm glad I was here, too. Goodnight, Jack, or, rather, good morning. I'll give you a call this afternoon." She walked into the corridor where, through the louvered glass, she could discern the first crimson rays of morning.

Katherine Kurtz

In "Vocation" Katherine Kurtz has presented a challenge which most of us would like to avoid. It is easy to see ourselves as Gilrae sees himself: victim of the universe without any real choice. What we don't want to face is that choices exist and it is within our power to make them. The only requirement, the price as it were, is that we take responsibility for the choice. To accept responsibility is to be willing to shoulder the burden and to realize that there will be consequences. I cannot make one choice without eliminating others, but we can make choices that open ever greater options or choices that limit us. *How* to choose is as much a choice as *what* to choose.

This story asks us to give up the superficial notion that the rich or powerful are necessarily freer than the poor or downtrodden. Gilrae is not free until he makes the choice to be free—and accepts the responsibility inherent in that choice. Freedom is not to be confused with license or with independence; it can entail intense commitment and can require total discipline and obedience. This is the freedom which is spoken of in the Scripture: "You shall know the truth, and the truth shall make you free" (John 8:32).

There are people in the world who seem able to take any situation, no matter how poor, and turn it to advantage. It is easy to stand on the outside, looking in, and envy their "luck," ignoring the sheer hard work and the willingness those people have to take a deep breath and start over, not once, but again and again. We would do well to realize how much of their luck is a result of being willing to make choices and accept consequences.

Miss Kurtz asks us to lay aside willingly those behaviors which limit us, to accept the demands of a life of true freedom . . . to seek broader horizons and higher goals. She asks us to turn with joy and answer, as Gilrae answers, "*Adsum!*"

· Katherine Kurtz ·

VOCATION

The air was cold and very still as Gilrae, the doomed young heir d'Eirial, reined in his mare at the top of the rise and glanced back the way he had come. He and his mount cast only an odd, truncated shadow on the virgin snow, for the sun was as high overhead as it was like to get on this bright winter day, but crisp, dainty hoofprints stretched back clearly to the point where he had left the main track. Few would dare to follow, for the ruins ahead were believed by most folk to be haunted, but Caprus would have no trouble finding him, if he really wanted to. Caprus had always made it his business to know the whereabouts of his elder half-brother—groomed by his mother from birth to be alert to faults which might turn their father's favor from the son of his first marriage to that of his second. If only Caprus could believe how little his supposed rival sought their father's title—or how little time there was before the title passed again: brother to brother, the next time, instead of father to son.

But Gilrae's last ordeal still lay months in the future. Their father's was in progress, and Gilrae could no longer bear to watch it happening. For the next few hours, Caprus and his mother could keep the death watch without him; they would not miss him anyway, until the old man was dead. And in whatever time remained before Caprus came to fetch him, Gilrae must weigh his own soul's yearnings and reach some firm decision. At least the air was clean here at the crest of the Lendours. He did not think he could have borne the closeness of his father's sickroom for another minute.

Gilrae's sigh hung on the frosty air as he touched heels to the mare and urged her up onto the plateau, letting her choose her own footing as he turned his attention to the ruined walls coming into sight. In addition to the initial destruction wreaked on the abbey and its inhabitants, the decay of more than half a century of hard winters and neglect had taken heavy toll. The scavenging of local crofters had compounded the process, for the smooth blue ashlars from the outer walls made sturdy hearths and cottage walls and even sheep pens for those bold enough to risk the ghosts and strong enough to cart them away. In some spots, little remained of the outer walls besides foundations.

Gilrae thought about the ghosts as the mare minced her way across a broken, ice-slick courtyard, her ears lacing back at a rabbit that broke from cover. He supposed it was inevitable that the place should have fostered such fears. Even before its fall, Saint Neot's had been rife with forbidden magic. Deryni sorcery had been its mainstay—sorcery which the Church condemned as evil, its practitioners anathema. To be Deryni was to live under sentence of death, if one did not renounce one's hell-born powers and adopt a life of penance and submission. That these particular Deryni were said to have been healers and teachers of healers was immaterial, for the healing had come of their misbegotten powers, and hence from the Devil—or so the priests taught. The abbey's destroyers, crack troops of the young king's regents, had slaughtered the monks to a man, and their students as well, profaning the holy chapel with a sea of blood and desecrating the altar itself with vicious murder.

Nor had that been the extent of the raiders' savagery. When they had finished their brutal butcher's work and sacked the abbey of its portable wealth, they set upon a systematic destruction of what they could not carry off, smashing the leaded glass and the fine carvings which adorned altar screens and choir stalls and chapel doorways, scarring the tougher stone with sword and mace blows, and then torching the lot. Rare manuscripts of human crafting, as well as heretical Deryni works, went to feed the flames which licked at the oak-beamed ceilings, the roof thatching. When, two days later, the fires at last burned out, men with ropes and horses pulled down what the flames had spared. More than half a century later, few walls stood higher than the withers of Gilrae's mount. In the face of such mayhem, small wonder that the local folk feared the vengeance of Deryni ghosts.

Gilrae had never met any of those ghosts, of course. Nor, to his knowledge, had he even met a Deryni, ghost or otherwise, though the priests warned that the sorcerers were devious, and one could never be too sure. Even the places formerly inhabited by such men were to be shunned, the priests said—though Gilrae had not known that as a young boy; and as an adult, he had years of personal experience to tell him that they must be wrong about this particular place. There was surely no evil here. And as for ghosts—

Ghosts, indeed! As Gilrae guided his mare through what remained of gatehouse and porter's lodge, nearing what once had been the cellar level of a dormitory block, he remembered the one conversation he and old Simonn had had about the alleged ghosts—and the chuckle and look of bemused indulgence he had gotten for his trouble.

Well, the old man certainly ought to know. He had been living in these ruins, in defiance of ghosts and skittish priests, since Gilrae's father was a boy. If there *were* ghosts, they had never bothered Simonn—or Gilrae.

But mental debates on the existence of ghosts were not conducive to watching where one was going. The mare knew, but Gilrae had not been to the ruins since before his accident, and he had forgotten the depth of the drop as the mare jumped down to the level of the former cellar—a leap not much farther than the height of the mare's belly, but Gilrae was unprepared, and his right hand gave when he tried to brace himself in old reflex. The jolt threw him against the front of the saddle so hard that he all but lost his seat. The pain which shot up his arm from wrist to shoulder nearly made him faint.

He rode the remaining distance in tight-lipped silence, head bowed in the shadow of his fur-lined cap, useless right hand wedged into the front opening of his leather riding jerkin to keep it from flapping around. When he reached the alcove he often used as a makeshift stable, he dismounted easily enough; but when he tried to loosen the girth, he found he could not do it left-handed. Biting back tears of anger and frustration, he gave the mare an apologetic pat on the neck and turned away, scrambling over the snow-covered rubble toward the open cloister garth. His sword, awkward and unwieldy hanging from his right side rather than his left, kept banging against his boots and tangling between his legs as he climbed up to the cloister level, nearly tripping him several times and bringing the hot tears to his eyes despite his determination to the contrary. The footing was better in the open, though, and he tried to put aside his bitterness as he emerged into sunlight.

The place brought back happier memories. As a boy, he could remember stealing away here for hours at a time: pretending that the ruined church was whole, and he free to choose, never even dreaming that the choices would be taken from him before he could even make them.

He had longed to be a priest even then. As a very young boy, he had even dared to pretend he *was* a priest, and had often played at celebrating Mass with an acorn-cap chalice and an oak-leaf paten. When he had shyly confided it to the old priest who was his tutor and chaplain, and asked whether he might one day become a priest in fact, the old man had sputtered and ranted and given him a stiff penance—not only for the sacrilege of pretending the sacrifice of the Mass, but for even thinking of the priesthood when he was the lord's eldest son. The Church might be for younger sons of noble families, but not for the heir. Old

Father Erdic had even told his father, in blatant defiance of the seal of the confessional.

His father's response had been predictable and harsh: a birch rod applied liberally to Gilrae's bare buttocks and a week of seclusion in his room, with only bread and water. Months had passed before Gilrae found a way to slip away alone again, and he had never again trusted the forsworn priest. Nor had he given up his acorn and leaf Masses, at least for a while, though in time the futility of it all relegated the practice to only a childhood memory.

He caught himself smiling as he remembered those days of youthful innocence, wondering that he ever could have been so naive. He was twenty now. He was still the heir d'Eirial, and could become baron at any moment. The previous Easter, he had been knighted by King Uthyr himself, who had addressed him as Right Trusty and Well-Beloved, in anticipation of his imminent inheritance. Any ordinary man should have been content; but all Gilrae d'Eirial had ever really wanted was to be a priest.

No longer smiling, he turned slow, reluctant steps across the open space of the cloister garth and headed toward what remained of the chapel, avoiding the rougher going of the peripheral walks, with their litter of charred beams and fallen stones. Fresh sheep droppings confirmed the identity of the last living things to pass this way, but of other humans there was no trace. Balancing precariously with only one good hand to steady him, Gilrae made his way up broken, snow-slick steps to pause in the shelter of a once-grand processional doorway, blowing on his gloved fist to warm it as he surveyed the south transept and crossing and eastern nave. Only the expected sheep were browsing in the ruins, nibbling at lichens and tufts of frost-seared grass.

Removing his cap, for he liked to think of the place as holy still, he moved on through the transept in the direction of the choir, musing again on the place's past. Saint Neot's had fallen, they said, in the same year good King Cinhil died—the year the bishops had condemned the Deryni as a race and declared them anathema, to be shunned, persecuted, and often even slaughtered by righteous men because of what they were. It had been on a Christmas eve a full three-score years ago—sixty years ago *today*, Gilrae realized, as he did the necessary arithmetic in his head.

The sun chose that moment to go behind a cloud, plunging Gilrae and the ruined choir aisle into shadow, and he shivered. In the heavy atmosphere of his father's sickroom, he had nearly forgotten that it was Christmas eve. Many people believed that the anniversaries of terrible events held powerful potential for supernatural visitations—and what place more likely than an altar profaned by murder?

Still chilled by more than cold, he cast a nervous glance in the direction of the desecrated altar. The previous night's snowfall had given it new altar coverings, disguising the vast cracks across the once-hallowed slab, but as the sun re-emerged, the illusion became apparent. The battered edges spoke all too clearly of the violence and the hate of its destroyers, and suddenly Gilrae felt an almost irresistible urge to sign himself in protection—an inclination immediately thwarted by his useless right hand.

Angry, both at his helplessness and at the superstition which had brought it to mind again, he dashed recklessly up the choir, sword flailing at his side as he plunged and stumbled through the snow. His bravado deserted him as he reached the foot of the altar steps, however. Sobbing for breath, he dropped to both knees on the lowest step and buried his face in his good hand.

Everything was denied him now. Once there had been choices, had he but had the nerve to make them; but now, either path he once might have traveled was barred to him. Even were it not for the malignant growth paralyzing his arm, even if there had only been the accident—if he could not wield a sword with a useless right hand, neither could he function as a priest. The Church kept strict standards for the fitness of priestly candidates, and a man who could not properly handle the Mass vessels at the time he sought ordination certainly would not be accepted.

With vision blurred by tears which would no longer be denied, Gilrae yanked at the ties of his fur-lined cloak until he could pull it off and spread it leather side down on a relatively dry patch of unbroken flags just at the foot of the altar steps. He hardly noticed the warmth of the sun on his back as he prostrated himself on the thick, wolfskin pelt, too numb with grief and loss to do more than lie there weeping bitterly for several minutes, forehead cradled in his good arm. Despair shifted to resentment after a while—an angry, defiant argument with God, protesting the gross unfairness of it all, pleading for reprieve—and then contrition for his presumption.

Very well. If he was meant to die with neither life fulfilled, then at least let *that* be to the glory of the One he would far rather have served in other ways. Setting himself to formal prayer, he admitted his terror of what lay ahead and offered it up, pleading for the strength to accept what was ordained. When even that brought no comfort, he let himself drift in numb dejection and tried not to think at all, the sun on his back gradually lulling the last of his terror to resignation.

For a while, only the swirling colors played behind his closed eyelids; but then, with a bright clarity which he had only occasionally experienced before, images began to form behind his eyes.

In his altered vision, it seemed that the abbey walls rose around him once more, the high, mosaic-lined vaulting of the choir dome arching protectively over his vantage point. The sanctuary shone with candlelight, the pale, carved wood of the choir stalls restored, the ruby glow of a Presence lamp above the high altar lending the snow-white walls a pinkish tint.

The abbey was peopled once more, as well, by silent, white-robed men with single braids emerging from under the cowls which fell back upon their shoulders. He sensed them approaching from the processional door, their double file splitting around him to enter the choir stalls to either side. Turning toward the altar as one man, they made their obeisance in perfect unison, raising their voices in the most beautiful harmony Gilrae had ever heard. Only the first few words were distinct, but they brought back all the poignance of the life to which Gilrae now would never dare aspire.

Adsum Domine . . . . Here am I, Lord . . . .

It was also the response of the candidate for priesthood as he presented himself before his ordaining bishop—words which Gilrae now would never speak.

The anguish which welled up anew in his chest blotted out the vision, and muffling a sob, he rolled onto his side and then to a sitting position to cradle his throbbing arm. Only then did he become aware that he was not alone, and whirled around on the seat of his leather britches, good hand going for the dagger at his belt.

But even as he turned, he realized that if the intruder had wished him harm, he could have been dead several times over. In any case, the old man sitting on a stone block a few feet away posed no threat. With an uneasy grin, Gilrae let the dagger slip back into its sheath and sat up straighter, surreptitiously dragging his left sleeve across his face, though he pretended only to brush a lock of hair out of his eyes. He should have expected the visit, after seeing the sheep. He hoped the old man had not noticed he'd been crying.

"Simonn. You startled me. I thought I was alone."

"I shall leave, if you wish," the man replied.

"No. Don't go."

"Very well."

No one knew who old Simonn was, or where he had come from. He had been old when Gilrae's father had played here as a boy. He tended his sheep, sometimes trading their wool for necessities in the spring; occasionally, he came down to the village church to hear Mass. Simonn the shepherd, Simonn the hermit, Simonn the holy man, some said. Gilrae had discovered quite by accident that the old man could read and write—a skill not easily or often gained by peasants, especially here in the Lendour highlands. Gilrae himself had had to fight for the privilege, and he the lord's son. He had never presumed on their friendship by inquiring too insistently, but he sometimes wondered how much more Simonn was than he appeared. Whoever he was, he had always been a friend to Gilrae.

The old man smiled and nodded, almost as if he had been aware of Gilrae's inner dialogue, but the blue eyes were kindly and unthreatening as they gazed across the short distance between them. When Gilrae did not speak, Simonn raised a white eyebrow and made gentle clucking noises with his tongue.

"So, young Master Gilrae, I've not seen you in many months. What brings you to the hills on this bright Christmas eve? I should have thought you would be feasting in your father's hall, preparing to welcome the Christ Child."

Gilrae hung his head. It was obvious the old man had not heard, either of his father's illness or his own misfortune. He could feel the wild pulse throbbing through the growth of his inner forearm as he cradled it closer to his midriff. The thought of the two coming deaths, his father's and his own, made his stomach queasy.

"There will be no feasting in Haut Eirial this night, Simonn," he whispered. "My father is dying. I—had to get away for a few hours."

"Ah, I see," the old man said, after a slight pause. "And you are feeling the weight of your coming responsibility."

Gilrae said nothing. If only it were that simple. With two good hands, he supposed he could have resigned himself to the life of a secular lord, governing the d'Eirial lands and keeping the king's peace, as his father wanted. With two good hands, he might even have had the courage to give it all up in favor of his brother, and make the choice he had longed to make for years. But the accident, and the resultant *thing* growing in his arm, had put an end to choices.

He shivered as he inadvertently clutched it closer, instinctively protective of what he feared the most, but despite old Simonn's watchful eyes, he was unable to suppress a grimace as pain shot up his arm. As he looked up defensively, daring the old man to mention it, Simonn casually turned toward the ruined altar, his face going very quiet.

"It is not an easy thing to lose what one loves," Simonn murmured after a moment, apparently testing. "Nor is it ever an easy thing to shoulder responsibilities, even if one welcomes them. And if one finds oneself forced into responsibilities by circumstances, rather than by a choice based on love, the task becomes even more difficult."

"Are you saying that I don't love my father?" Gilrae asked, after a stunned pause.

Simonn shook his head. "Of course not. I think you love him very much, as a son should love his father. If you did not, you would not now be agonizing over the choices you must make. We rarely *ask* for the choices which are placed before us, but they must always be made, nonetheless."

Swallowing with difficulty, Gilrae turned his gaze to the wolf-skin lining of the cloak he sat on, unconsciously rubbing his numb right arm to warm it.

"What—makes you think I'm faced with any particular choices, old man?" he said, a little belligerently. "My father is dying, and I'm to be Baron d'Eirial. That involves no choices. It is a role I was born to."

"By blood—yes," Simonn replied. "But by spirit—well, I think you did not come to this ruined abbey while your father lay dying, and prostrate yourself before its altar, because you are overjoyed to be coming into your temporal inheritance. And I do not mean to imply that your grief at your father's passing is not genuine," he added, as Gilrae looked up in astonishment. "I wonder if you even know what drove you to present yourself this way—in this ruined church, before an altar drenched by the blood of scores of holy men."

Gilrae gave a sigh and lowered his eyes again, subdued. Simonn knew part of it, at least. It could not have been hard to guess. They had talked before, if only hypothetically, about the practical considerations of a religious life. Simonn had never quite said, but it was clear that, at least as a boy, he himself had received some kind of instruction in a religious community. Perhaps that was where he had learned to read and write.

"It doesn't matter anyway," Gilrae finally murmured. "The question is academic. There are no choices for me anymore—only duties and responsibilities which I'll be increasingly ill-equipped to handle. God, I almost wish I were dead already!"

Even as the bitter words left his lips, the shocked Simonn was on his feet and darting across the few feet which separated them, grabbing his wrist to shake him. It was the bad wrist, and Gilrae gasped aloud with the pain. Instantly, Simonn was kneeling beside him and shoving back his sleeve, pulling off the glove, running gentle fingers over the swollen flesh.

"How did this happen?" Simonn murmured, turning the forearm and drawing in breath as he spied the blackness spread along the inner side. "Why didn't you tell me you were ill?"

Gilrae swallowed and tried to pull away, feeling like an animal caught in a trap.

"Leave me alone. Please. What difference can it make?"

"It can mean your life!" the old man snapped, holding him with his eyes. "How did this start?"

"A—a fall from a horse, several months ago," Gilrae found himself saying. "I—thought it was only a bad sprain at first, but then the—swelling started."

"Have you much pain?"

Gilrae wrenched his gaze free with a gasp and nodded, staring unseeing at the ground.

"I—can't close my hand anymore, either," he managed to whisper. "I can't hold a sword, and I can't—"

Though he struggled to prevent it, the old dream flashed into memory again: himself, garbed in the vestments of a priest and raising the chalice at the celebration of the Mass. Choking back a sob, he shook his head to clear the image from his mind.

There *were* no choices now. That dream would never be; nor would he even be able to be a proper lord to his people. All the doors were closing. Until now, he had never even thought about ending his life before the blackness could, but perhaps he *would* be better off.

"What else can't you do?" old Simonn urged softly, the voice boring into his brain. "What is it you *really* want most?"

"I want another chance, I suppose," Gilrae whispered after a moment, dropping his head to rest his forehead on his knees, no longer minding that his arm still lay in Simonn's hands. "I want it to be last spring, when I was still a whole man, and the decisions were still mine to make. All the choices have been made for me, now. I'll die from this. No one else knows about that part of it except my father's battle surgeon, but it's going to happen." He lifted his head to glance at the useless arm with tear-blurred eyes. "I lacked the courage to follow my own heart when I still had the chance—and now I can't even follow my father's heart and be a worthy leader for his people, once he's gone."

He found himself staring stupidly into space for a while, but then Simonn's soft sigh was bringing him back.

"I can't help you with your decisions, Gilrae, but I might be able to help you with your arm," the old man said. "It would be rather painful, but the growth could be removed."

Gilrae swallowed noisily, afraid to let himself dare to hope.

"I'd like to believe you, but I don't think so," he managed to murmur. "Gilbert said it would only come back, worse than before, and that it would spread. The arm could be cut off—that *might* stop it, *if* I survived the amputation—but what good would that do? It wouldn't allow either of the lives I'd choose, if the choices still were mine."

"We always have choices, Son," Simonn replied, in a voice so soft and yet so compelling that Gilrae turned to look at him again. "If you choose to let me try to help you, I may be able to make it possible for you to reopen those other choices. What do you have to lose?"

And what, indeed, *did* he have to lose? Gilrae reasoned, as he stared into the old man's eyes and found himself swaying dizzily. As if some force outside himself compelled his movement, he felt his left hand going to the knife at his belt and unsheathing it, handing the blade across to Simonn hilt first, rising at the old man's beckoning gesture to pull his cloak around himself and mount the altar steps behind him.

"Sit here," the old man whispered, pulling him toward the left-hand corner and setting his back against the cold marble.

Gilrae felt his knees buckle under him, and his back slid slowly down the stone facade until he was sitting, surrounded by the folds of the fur-lined cloak, his sword lying close along his right thigh. Snow still lay in drifts in the north shadow of the altar, and he could not seem to resist as Simonn pushed back the sleeve of his leather tunic and buried the right forearm in the snow to numb it further. The sun was more than halfway down the western sky—how *had* it gotten so late already—but its light still dazzled Gilrae's eyes as he laid his head against the marble behind him, golden fire also flashing from the blade Simonn polished on a surprisingly clean hem of pale grey undertunic.

When the cold of the snow against his arm began to ache more than the original pain, Simonn turned the forearm upward in its bed of melting snow and ran a hand over the area to be excised.

"You needn't watch this," he said, touching ice-cold fingers to the side of Gilrae's face to turn his head away. "Look out at the sunset and think about other things. Watch the clouds, if you like. Perhaps the shapes will suggest answers to your questions."

The old man's fingers seemed somehow to numb Gilrae's brain as well as the flesh they touched, and he found himself becoming very detached from his still body. As Simonn bent over the up-turned forearm and positioned his blade, Gilrae summoned just enough will to glance down and see the steel trace a crimson path along one side of the blackness he had come to hate and fear. The blood welled up scarlet against the snow, steaming in the frigid air, and Gilrae rolled his eyes upward again to gaze at the sky. After a few seconds more, his eyes closed and he dreamed.

He was in a church again, but it was smaller than the one he had seen before—no more than a chapel, really—and this time, he was a participant rather than an observer: one of four solemn yet joyful young men in white, processing down the narrow nave.

Like the others, he carried a lighted candle in his right hand; his left was pressed reverently to the deacon's stole crossing his chest and secured at his right hip. The men in the single row of stalls to either side wore grey habits rather than the white of the previous dream, but a few of them sported the single braid Gilrae had noticed before. Ahead, at the foot of a far more humble altar, waited two men in copes and mitres.

He knelt with his brethren at their feet—a bishop and a mitred abbot, he somehow knew—and though he could not quite make out the words the senior of them spoke, he knew the response. He and his brethren sang it together as they held their candles aloft, the notes floating pure and clear in that holy place.

Adsum, Domine . . . . Here am I, Lord . . . .

The scene wavered and dissolved at that, much to his regret, and for an indeterminable while he simply floated a little sadly in a state of disconnection, only dimly aware of the sunlight on his face, beating on his closed eyelids, and the cold penetrating his cloak and riding leathers from the stone step, the altar at his back, the snow still numbing his right arm past all feeling.

He had no inclination to open his eyes, to move, or even to think. He drifted some more—and then he was back in the dream, humbly kneeling with joined hands before the bishop, swaying a little on his knees as the consecrated hands came to rest on his head.

Accipe Spiritum Sanctum . . .

He imagined he could feel the holy power surging through every nerve and sinew, the Divine energy filling him to overflowing and then opening him to fill even more. The ecstasy grew so intense that he began to tremble.

Then, suddenly, he was aware of cold hands on either side of his face, and old Simonn's voice gently bidding him open his eyes. He managed to make his dry throat contract in a swallow, but he was still disoriented for a moment, and could not quite seem to bring Simonn into focus.

"I—you—"

"You're all right. I think you must have fallen asleep on me," the old man murmured, smiling. "Did you dream?"

"I did. How did you know? Simonn, it was wonderful! I—"

Confused, Gilrae raised both hands to rub his temples before he realized that the right hand had obeyed just like the left one, and that there was no longer any pain. A strip of grey cloth bound his right arm from wrist halfway to elbow, but no unnatural bulge disturbed the clean line. Blood stained the snow where his arm had lain, but far less than he might have expected. Simonn was retrieving his dagger even as Gilrae started to speak, burnishing the melted snow from blade and grip and extending it to him hilt-first.

"I believe your father's battle surgeon may have frightened you unduly," the old man said. "It shouldn't come back. You may still have some weakness for a few days, but I think you'll find that you can grip a sword—or anything else you may wish."

"But—"

Simonn shook his head and held up a hand to stop his question, then stood and shaded his eyes against the sun, gazing west beyond the ruins. As Gilrae, too, scrambled to his feet, steadying himself on the corner of the altar, Simonn began kicking fresh snow over the bloodstains at their feet, erasing the visible evidence of what had just occurred.

"Your brother is coming, and an escort with him," Simonn said, glancing up at him as he finished the job. "I fear he brings news which will sadden you—but at least you may now make your decisions based on what you really want, not on what your physical condition seemed to dictate. If you value what I have done, say nothing of my part in this, I beg you."

"You have my word," Gilrae promised.

But the old man was already gliding into the ruins, melting into the shadows, and so carefully had he chosen his escape route that even Gilrae, who had watched him go, could detect no sign of his passage.

His brother's voice called out his name then, and Gilrae knew it was only a matter of a few minutes before he was found. Scuttling around the ruined altar in a panic, hardly daring to believe, he crouched in its eastern shadow and tore at the bandage on his arm with trembling fingers, safe for a few more minutes from even Caprus's prying eyes. Beneath the bandage, only a yellowed shadow of former bruising showed where once the fatal blackness had spread—that and a faint pink line where he thought his blade had gone. Of the growth there was no trace.

Amazed, he flexed his fingers and made a fist, watching the tendons ripple under the skin, feeling the muscles obey. A growing suspicion nagged at the edges of his mind about old Simonn, but the healing spoke for itself. He would worry later about its source—and the promise of the dream. For now, it was sufficient that a miracle had occurred, and that he had been given back his choices.

"Lord Gilrae?"

The voice of Sir Lorcan, his father's seneschal, brought him back to earth with a jolt, and almost guiltily he tugged his sleeve back into place and dropped the bandage onto the snow. No time for contemplating miracles just now. As he struggled to pull fur-lined gloves onto damp hands, he could hear the hollow clip-clop of iron-shod hooves treading on the flagstones far back in the ruined nave, and the sound infuriated him.

Fools! Could they not sense that the ground was holy still? How dared they bring horses into this place?

Indignant at the manner of their intrusion, he hooked his right hand around the hilt of his sword and stood. He did not intend to tell them what had happened just yet. They spotted him as he moved around to the front of the altar to wait for them, Caprus pointing in his direction and urging the rest of them to follow faster. The horses plunged through the snow and slipped and scrambled on the uneven flags, scattering the sheep, their riders watching the footing now, instead of Gilrae.

They were ten in all, Caprus and Lorcan in the lead. Caprus wore a stormy look, for all the pale handsomeness of his bright yellow curls, and Lorcan's lined face was as grave as Gilrae had ever seen it. Father Arnulf and Master Gilbert, the surgeon, rode at their backs, and behind them half a dozen men-at-arms in his father's livery—*his* livery now, he suddenly realized. The men's short lances were reversed in the stirrup-rests, the silver circlet of his father's coronet clutched in the priest's gloved fist. Despite the fact that he had been expecting it, Gilrae suddenly felt very cold.

"Take the horses out of the church," he said quietly, when they reined in at the transept and started to dismount. "Don't argue, Lorcan, just do it."

He could sense Caprus's beginning indignation, but Lorcan murmured something sharply under his breath and turned his chestnut hard into the chest of Caprus's grey, shouldering it into a turn even as the surprised Caprus bit back whatever he had been about to say. Wordlessly the lot of them withdrew halfway along the length of the nave, where Lorcan, Caprus, and the priest and surgeon dismounted and gave their reins to the remaining men. As the horses were led out of the church, the four made their way back toward the altar on foot, muttering among themselves. Lorcan drew slightly ahead and bowed as he reached the foot of the altar steps. He was wearing mail and leathers beneath his fur-lined cloak, as were Caprus and the surgeon.

"I'm sorry, Lord Gilrae. Your father is dead," he said, his breath hanging on the chill air. "He bade us bring you this."

As he gestured slightly behind him, the middleaged Father Arnulf stepped forward and extended the coronet in unsteady hands.

"You are confirmed as the heir, my Lord," Arnulf said, a shadow of pity flickering behind his eyes as Gilrae reached out to touch the gleaming metal with his left hand only. "Since the king has already acknowledged it, in anticipation of this moment, there can be no question. May God bless you in your endeavors, my Lord."

Gilrae could sense the effort it took them not to look at his motionless right hand, but he still was not ready to reveal himself. With a nod to acknowledge all of them, he came slowly down the altar steps. Caprus was watching him with an expression of sorrow mixed with envy, Lorcan looking very uncomfortable. Only the staid Master Gilbert seemed unmoved by it all, though the brown eyes held compassion.

"I thank you, Father," Gilrae murmured, dropping to one knee before the priest. "Would you do me the favor of blessing my father's coronet before you place it on my head? I shall have many difficult decisions ahead of me from this time forward, and I shall surely need God's help to persevere."

Not even Caprus could dispute that. As the others knelt around him, warriors' harness clinking softly beneath riding leathers and furs, Gilrae bowed his head and let the priest's blessing roll over him like a wavelet on the lake at Dhassa, trying to think. The coronet across his forehead was cold and heavy, its weight far more than mere metal, pressing into his very soul as he stood and turned away from them, averting his eyes.

The time was come to make his decision. He was baron, but he now had the means to change that, if he dared. Retreating slowly to the altar, he spread his gloved left hand flat on the snow-covered mensa as if in oath, lifting the fingers of his right to brush the edge, shielded behind his body where the others could not see. As the fingers moved and he stared at them, he knew he had not been spared to wear a coronet.

"Sir Lorcan," he said softly, over his shoulder, "were you my father's liegeman?"

"My Lord, you know I was."

"And are you now my liegeman?"

"I am your man, my Lord," came the crisp reply.

"Thank you. Call the rest of the men here, if you please."

He continued to face the altar, but he could hear uneasy stirrings from Caprus's direction, and the low whisper of an exchange between Gilbert and the priest as Lorcan moved off a few paces to signal the men-at-arms to join them. When he sensed the arrival of the others, he drew deep breath and turned, very much aware of the weight of the circlet on his head. The men knelt in a semicircle at the foot of the steps, faces fiercely proud beneath their helmets. Caprus remained with the surgeon and the priest, looking vaguely uneasy as Lorcan moved halfway up the steps to bow.

"As you requested, my Lord."

"Yes, Thank you." Gilrae turned his eyes on the men gazing up at him. "Gentlemen, Sir Lorcan has confirmed his continued fealty to me as Baron d'Eirial. Have I your loyalty, as well?"

To murmurs of affirmation, the men drew their swords and held them toward him with the hilts uppermost, gauntleted hands grasping the naked blades just below the quillons. Gilrae nodded.

"Thank you. I take your actions as oaths sworn. You may stand, but remain where you are, please. Lorcan?"

"My Lord."

"Lorcan, I have need of your counsel. Caprus, please come forward."

As the men-at-arms rose and sheathed their weapons, and Lorcan moved silently to Gilrae's left elbow, Caprus came hesitantly to face his brother. He had blanched at the sound of his name, and his glove was tight across his knuckles where his left hand gripped the hilt of his sword as he walked. Wordlessly Gilrae came down the three steps from the altar, pausing where a snowbank stood knee high between them and motioning Caprus to join him. After a slight hesitation, Caprus obeyed, dropping uncertainly to one knee when Gilrae did not speak. Gilrae could sense Lorcan standing slightly behind him, but he did not take his eyes from his brother's. He did not know whether he would like the answer to the question he must now ask Caprus, but if he ever was to dare what his heart desired, an answer was demanded. He prayed God it would be the one he wanted to hear.

"How may I counsel you, my Lord?" Lorcan asked quietly.

"A point of jurisdiction. Have I the right, as Baron d'Eirial and a knight of this realm, to mete high and low justice in my lands, to all my vassals, great and small?"

"You do, my Lord."

High justice: the power of life and death. He had known it was so, but he had wanted to be sure. Before Caprus could do more than open his mouth to start to protest, Gilrae reached to his sword with his left hand and drew it hilt first, thrusting it into the snow between them like a javelin.

"Hold your peace, Caprus!" he snapped. "Keep silence and consider well what I am about to ask you. I have my reasons, and I swear I bear you no ill will."

Caprus was trembling with outrage, fists clenched rigidly at his sides, but he said nothing as his brother hooked his other hand in his sword belt and looked down at him. Despite Caprus's repeated mutterings of resentment all their lives about the succession, especially when his mother was around, Gilrae seriously doubted that Caprus had ever been actively disloyal, but he had to be certain—and, more important, his men must be certain. Though he once more had choices open to him, those choices also carried responsibilities.

"Caprus d'Eirial," he said clearly, "I require your solemn oath, before God and these assembled knights, that you have never, in word or in deed, acted against either me or our father to the detriment of our people."

Caprus's lower lip was trembling, but he met Gilrae's gaze squarely. Pride and anger played behind the pale blue eyes.

"How dare you ask such an oath?" he demanded. "And why, after speaking of the high justice? When have I ever given you cause to doubt my loyalty?"

"Place your hands on the sword and swear it, before God," Gilrae answered. "I am not required to tell you why. Only do it."

For one heart-stopping moment, Gilrae feared Caprus would refuse. The gravity of the question was apparent. But stiffnecked and arrogant as his younger brother sometimes was, Gilrae had never known him to be dishonest or forsworn. Could he not swallow his pride and give his oath?

"Swear it, Caprus," he repeated. "Please."

His faith was rewarded for the second time that afternoon, for all at once Caprus broke their defiant eye contact and yanked off both his gloves, laying bare hands firmly on the quillons, his thumbs resting on the center boss which concealed the sword's holy relics. The face he raised to Gilrae over the sword's cross hilt was tight-jawed, but otherwise expressionless.

"I swear before Almighty God and these assembled knights that I have always been loyal to our father and to you," Caprus said, the words clipped and precise. His gaze hardened, the jaw setting even more stubbornly, but then he seized the sword by its blade and jerked it from the snow, holding it aloft like a talisman between them as he went on.

"I do further swear, of my own free will and desire, that I am today become your liegeman of life and limb and of earthly worship. Faith and truth will I bear unto you, to live and to die, against all manner of folk, so help me God!" He paused to wet his lips uncertainly. "And if you think I ever would have played you false, you're wrong, Gilrae—regardless of what my mother might have had you believe. I was born your lawful brother, and you are now my lawful lord!"

He brought the blade to his lips and kissed the reliquary boss boldly enough, but when he held it out to Gilrae for the oath to be acknowledged, his gaze faltered a little—not with duplicity, but an honest fear that Gilrae might not believe he was sincere. Hardly able to contain his relief, Gilrae took back the sword in his left hand, just under the quillons, and glanced aside at the puzzled Lorcan.

"Sir Lorcan, one further question. Among my other prerogatives as baron, have I the right to create a knight?"

"A *knight*? Aye, my Lord, you do, but—"

As Lorcan moved a startled step closer, no less confused than the others murmuring among themselves, Gilrae shook his head and seized the hilt of his sword with his restored right hand, raising it blade upward in salute to kiss the relics in the hilt. A gasp rippled among them all, for Gilrae had not been able to do that since his fall. The stunned Caprus could only gape at him in astonishment, springing to his feet to grab at Gilrae's sword arm and push back the sleeve to stare.

"Gilrae, your arm—!" he began, genuine joy lighting the blue eyes.

Echoing Caprus's grin, Gilrae pressed his younger brother back to his knees with his free hand and glanced out at all of them, still holding the sword before him.

"Gentlemen, while I prayed this afternoon, something happened that I can't explain," he said quietly. "I was near despair because I thought all my choices had been taken from me. God saw fit to give me all my choices back." He smiled down at his brother. "I hope you will not think ill of me as I give over part of the burden to you, Caprus. I believe it is something you have long wanted, despite your love, and I know now that you will prove worthy of the test."

Before Caprus or any of the rest of them could even begin to question, Gilrae drew himself up formally and raised the sword, bringing the flat of the blade down smartly on Caprus's right shoulder.

"In the name of God and Saint Michael, I dub thee knight, Caprus d'Eirial," he said. The blade lifted to touch the left shoulder. "I give thee the right to bear arms and the duty to protect the weak and helpless."

He brought the blade to rest on Caprus's yellow curls, sighting down the gleaming blade to his brother's tear-bright eyes.

"I give thee also the charge of our father's lands and the meting of justice, high and low," he added, for an instant shifting his glance out over the awed men watching. "Be thou a good knight and gentle lord to these, thy people."

He drew the scabbard from his belt and sheathed the sword, then laid both across the astonished Caprus's hastily raised palms before taking the coronet from his head. He held it high in both his hands, so that there could be no mistaking his fitness for the honor he passed—and no mistaking his intent—then set it firmly on Caprus's head.

"Before God and these assembled witnesses, I renounce all claim to the lands and titles of Eirial, vesting them forever in this Caprus d'Eirial, my brother, trueborn son of the late Radulf d'Eirial, and his lawful descendants. This is my irrevocable intent, which I hope will be confirmed without question by our Lord the King."

Helping Caprus to his feet, right hand to right, he turned him to face the others. He wondered if his own contentment was as evident as Caprus's incredulous pleasure, and marveled that the choice could have seemed so difficult before.

"My Lords, I here present your new Baron d'Eirial. I command you to give him the same loyalty you gave our father, and which you earlier pledged to me. Do it. I haven't got all night."

Lorcan swore. The men swore. Master Gilbert swore, and even the priest swore. But as Caprus and the others moved off toward the horses, whispering excitedly among themselves and glancing back in awe, Lorcan lingered.

"But, what will you do now?" the old knight whispered, staring as Gilrae watched Caprus and the others disappear against the sunset glare. "You've given up everything, my Lord."

"I'm not your lord any longer, Lorcan—and I haven't given up anything that really mattered." Gilrae cocked his head at the other man. "Don't you understand? Before today, I had nothing. And then I was given everything, so that I might choose what I really wanted." He pulled off his right glove and laid his restored hand on the ruined altar.

"Don't you see? This is where I belong. Oh, not here, at this poor, ruined altar. I'm as stunned as you are, that a miracle could have taken place where magic once held sway. But maybe that means that the magic wasn't evil to begin with—I don't know. I do know that I'm not the same man I was when I came here earlier today."

Closing his hand as if to cup something precious, he gazed beyond the altar to where a Presence lamp had burned in his dream.

"I think I've been given a sign, Lorcan—one that I can finally comprehend. It's what I was always looking for—you know that. I don't intend to throw away my second chance."

The old knight shook his head. "You're right. I don't understand." He snorted, then stuck out his hand, which Gilrae took. "If you've found your vocation, though, I pray God will prosper you, my Lord."

"Not 'my Lord' anymore, Lorcan. Just Gilrae—and maybe *Father* Gilrae someday, if what I pray is true."

"And if it isn't?"

"I think it is," he said with a smile. A slight movement had caught his eye off in the north transept, and he gave Lorcan's hand a final squeeze.

"You'd better go now, old friend. Your new lord is waiting, as is mine. Serve Caprus faithfully, as you would have served me. I have no doubt you'll find him worthy."

The old knight did not speak, but as he bowed over his former master's hand in farewell, he pressed his lips against its back in final homage, battle-scarred fingers briefly caressing the smooth flesh of the once swollen wrist. Then he was turning on his heel and striding down the steps, head ducked down in the collar of his cloak, stumbling a little as he receded down the nave.

Gilrae stared after him, sun-dazzled, then drew on his glove again and turned to lay his hands on the ruined altar once more, bowing his head in blind and wordless thanksgiving. He felt the sun die behind him, and the deepening shadows of the evening, and after a while longer, the touch of a hand on his right shoulder.

"Gilrae?"

"*Adsum,*" Gilrae whispered.

Old Simonn's gentle chuckle floated on the air like music as the night's first snowflakes began to drift to earth. Out on the eastern horizon, Gilrae realized that the evening's first star was heralding a personal advent, as well as the coming of the Christmas King.

"Come, young friend," came Simonn's invitation. "But you must save that word for another than myself. Come and I'll take you to an unstained altar."

Stephen R. Donaldson

I have some verses of Sir Thomas Browne on my wall as a constant reminder:

> If thou could'st empty all thyself of self,
> Like to a shell dishabited,
> Then might He find thee on the ocean shelf,
> And say, "This is not dead,"
> And fill thee with Himself instead.
> But thou are all replete with very thou
> And hast such shrewd activity,
> That when He comes He says, "This is enow
> Unto itself—'twere better let it be,
> It is so small and full, there is no room for Me."

As a Christian, it is important that I try to empty myself of self so that there can be room for God to work in me and through me. I cannot serve as a channel to other lives when I am "replete with very me," for all I can give then is ME—nothing greater, nothing stronger. Emptying oneself, however, is only part of what is needed—as Donaldson reminds us in this story. We must also remember that it is not in the nature of God to force himself on us in any way; the God revealed in Scripture is not one who usurps my free will. He will ask—sometimes more than once—but it is always my choice to accept or reject the request. I cannot be used as an instrument unless I first give permission.

If we are to stand on the side of good, we must be sensitive to the requests that will be made of our lives. God will not manipulate us. Of what worth is love when it is compelled? We love because we first were loved, but our love must be freely given, we must choose freely to participate in relationship.

George Hodges says, "God calls us to duty, and the only right answer is obedience. God calls. It is better to obey blunderingly than not to obey at all." And William Ullathorne adds, "The test of love is not feeling, but obedience."

· Stephen R. Donaldson ·

UNWORTHY
OF THE ANGEL

"Let no man be unworthy of the Angel
who stands over him."
—Unknown

—and stumbled when my feet seemed to come down on the sidewalk out of nowhere. The heat was like walking into a wall; for a moment, I couldn't find my balance. Then I bumped into somebody. That kept me from falling. But he was a tall man in an expensive suit, certain and pitiless, and his expression as he recoiled said plainly that people like me shouldn't be allowed out on the streets.

I retreated until I could brace my back against the hard glass of a display window and tried to take hold of myself. It was always like this; I was completely disoriented—a piece of cork carried down the river. Everything seemed to be melting from one place to another. Back and forth in front of me, people with bitten expressions hurried, chasing disaster. In the street, too many cars snarled and blared at each other, blaming everything except themselves. The buildings seemed to go up for miles into a sky as heavy as a lid. They looked elaborate and hollow, like crypts.

And the heat—! I couldn't see the sun, but it was up there somewhere, in the first half of the morning, hidden by humidity and filth. Breathing was like inhaling hot oil. I had no idea where I was; but wherever it was, it needed rain.

Maybe I didn't belong here. I prayed for that. The people who flicked glances at me didn't want what they saw. I was wearing a grey overcoat streaked with dust, spotted and stained. Except for a pair of ratty shoes, splitting at the seams, and my clammy pants, the coat was all I had on. My face felt like I'd spent the night in a pile of trash. But if I had, I couldn't remember. Without hope, I put my hands in all my pockets, but they were empty. I didn't have a scrap of identification or money to make things easier. My only hope was that everything still seemed to be melting. Maybe it would melt into something else, and I would be saved.

But while I fought the air and the heat and prayed, Please, God, not again, the entire street sprang into focus without warning. The sensation snatched my weight off the glass, and I turned in time to see a young woman emerge from the massive building that hulked beside the storefront where I stood.

She was dressed with the plainness of somebody who didn't have any choice—the white blouse gone dingy with use, the skirt fraying at the hem. Her fine hair, which deserved better, was efficiently tied at the back of her neck. Slim and pale, too pale, blinking at the heat, she moved along the sidewalk to pass in front of the store. Her steps were faintly unsteady, as if she were worn out by the burden she carried.

She held a handkerchief to her face like a woman who wanted to disguise the fact that she was still crying.

She made my heart clench with panic. While she passed in front of me, too absorbed in her distress to notice me or anyone else, I thought she was the reason I was here.

But after that first spasm of panic, I followed her. She seemed to leave waves of urgency on either side, and I was pulled along in her wake.

The crowds slowed me down. I didn't catch up with her until she reached the corner of the block and stopped to wait for the light to change. Some people pushed out into the street anyway;

cars screamed at them until they squeezed back onto the sidewalk. Everybody was in a hurry, but not for joy. The tension and the heat daunted me. I wanted to hold back—wanted to wait until she found her way to a more private place. But she was as distinct as an appeal in front of me, a figure etched in need. And I was only afraid.

Carefully, almost timidly, I reached out and put my hand on her arm.

Startled, she turned toward me; her eyes were wide and white, flinching. For an instant, her protective hand with the handkerchief dropped from the center of her face, and I caught a glimpse of what she was hiding.

It wasn't grief.

It was blood.

It was vivid and fatal, stark with implications. But I was still too confused to recognize what it meant.

As she saw what I looked like, her fright receded. Under other circumstances, her face might have been soft with pity. I could tell right away that she wasn't accustomed to being so lost in her own needs. But now they drove her, and she didn't know what to do with me.

Trying to smile through my dirty whiskers, I said as steadily as I could, "Let me help you."

But as soon as I said it, I knew I was lying. She wasn't the reason I was here.

The realization paralysed me for a moment. If she'd brushed me off right then, there would've been nothing I could do about it. She wasn't the reason—? Then why had I felt such a shock of importance when she came out to the street? Why did her nose-bleed—which really didn't look very serious—seem so fatal to me? While I fumbled with questions, she could've simply walked away from me.

But she was near the limit of her courage. She was practically frantic for any kind of assistance or comfort. But my appearance was against me. As she clutched her handkerchief to her nose again, she murmured in surprise and hopelessness, "What're you talking about?"

That was all the grace I needed. She was too vulnerable to turn her back on any offer, even from a man who looked like me. But I could see that she was so fragile now because she had been so brave for so long. And she was the kind of woman who didn't turn her back. That gave me something to go on.

"Help is the circumference of need," I said. "You wouldn't be feeling like this if there was nothing anybody could do about it. Otherwise the human race would've committed suicide two days after Adam and Eve left the Garden."

I had her attention now. But she didn't know what to make of me. She wasn't really listening to herself as she murmured, "You're wrong." She was just groping. "I mean your quote. Not help. Reason. 'Reason is the circumference of energy.' Blake said that."

I didn't know who Blake was, but that didn't matter. She'd given me permission—enough permission, anyway, to get me started. I was still holding her arm, and I didn't intend to let her go until I knew why I was here—what I had to do with her.

Looking around for inspiration, I saw we were standing in front of a coffee shop. Through its long glass window, I saw that it was nearly empty; most of its patrons had gone looking for whatever they called salvation. I turned back to the woman and gestured toward the shop. "I'll let you buy me some coffee if you'll tell me what's going on."

She was in so much trouble that she understood me. Instead of asking me to explain myself, she protested, "I can't. I've got to go to work. I'm already late."

Sometimes it didn't pay to be too careful. Bluntly, I said, "You can't do that, either. You're still bleeding."

At that, her eyes widened; she was like an animal in a trap. She hadn't thought as far ahead as work. She had come out onto the sidewalk without one idea of what she was going to do. "Reese—," she began, then stopped to explain. "My brother." She looked miserable. "He doesn't like me to come home when he's working. It's too important. I didn't even tell him I was going to the doctor." Abruptly, she bit herself still, distrusting the impulse or instinct that drove her to say such things to a total stranger.

Knots of people continued to thrust past us, but now their vehemence didn't touch me. I hardly felt the heat. I was locked to this woman who needed me, even though I was almost sure she wasn't the one I was meant to help. Still smiling, I asked, "What did the doctor say?"

She was too baffled to refuse. "He didn't understand it. He said I shouldn't be bleeding. He wanted to put me in the hospital. For observation."

"But you won't go," I said at once.

"I can't." Her whisper was nearly a cry. "Reese's show is tomorrow. His first big show. He's been living for this all his life. And he has so much to do. To get ready. If I went to the hospital, I'd have to call him. Interrupt—. He'd have to come to the hospital."

Now I had her. When the necessity is strong enough—and when I've been given enough permission—I can make myself obeyed. I let go of her arm and held out my hand. "Let me see that handkerchief."

Dumbly, as if she were astonished at herself, she lowered her hand and gave me the damp cloth.

It wasn't heavily soaked; the flow from her nose was slow. That was why she was able to even consider the possibility of going to work. But her red pain was as explicit as a wail in my hand. I watched a new bead of blood gather in one of her nostrils, and it told me a host of things I was not going to be able to explain to her. The depth of her peril and innocence sent a jolt through me that nearly made me fold at the knees. I knew now that she was not the person I had been sent here to help. But she was the reason. Oh, she was the *reason*, the victim whose blood cried out for intervention. Sweet Christ, how had she let this be done to her?

But then I saw the way she held her head up while her blood trickled to her upper lip. In her eyes, I caught a flash of the kind of courage and love that got people into trouble because it didn't count the cost. And I saw something else, too—a hint that on some level, intuitively, perhaps even unconsciously, she understood what was happening to her. So naturally she refused to go to the hospital. No hospital could help her.

I gave the handkerchief back to her gently, though inside I was trembling with anger. The sun beat down on us. "You don't need a doctor," I said as calmly as I could. "You need to buy me some coffee and tell me what's going on."

She still hesitated. I could hardly blame her. Why should she want to sit around in a public place with a handkerchief held to her nose? But something about me had reached her, and it wasn't my brief burst of authority. Her eyes went down my coat to my shoes; when they came back up, they were softer. Behind her hand, she smiled faintly. "You look like you could use it."

She was referring to the coffee; but it was her story I intended to use.

She led the way into the coffee shop and toward one of the booths; she even told the petulant waiter what we wanted. I appreciated that. I really had no idea where I was. In fact, I didn't so much as know what coffee was. But sometimes knowledge comes to me when I need it. I didn't even blink as the waiter dropped heavy cups in front of us, sloshing hot, black liquid onto the table. Instead I concentrated everything I had on my companion.

When I asked her, she said her name was Kristen Dona. Following a hint I hadn't heard anybody give me, I looked at her left hand and made sure she wasn't wearing a wedding ring. Then I said to get her started, "Your brother's name is Reese. This has something to do with him."

"Oh, no," she said quickly. Too quickly. "How could it?" She wasn't lying. She was just telling me what she wanted to believe.

I shrugged. There was no need to argue with her. Instead, I let the hints lead me. "He's a big part of your life," I said as if we were talking about the weather. "Tell me about him."

"Well—." She didn't know where to begin. "He's a sculptor. He has a show tomorrow—I told you that. His first big show. After all these years."

I studied her closely. "But you're not happy about it."

"Of course I am!" She was righteously indignant. And under that, she was afraid. "He's worked so hard—! He's a good sculptor. Maybe even a great one. But it isn't exactly easy. It's not like being a writer—he can't just go to a publisher and have them print a hundred thousand copies of his work for two ninety-five. He has to have a place where people who want to spend money on art can come and see what he does. And he has to charge a lot because each piece costs him so much time and effort. So a lot of people have to see each piece before he can sell one. That means he has to have shows. In a gallery. This is his first real chance."

For a moment, she was talking so hotly that she forgot to cover her nose. A drop of blood left a mark like a welt across her lip.

Then she felt the drop and scrubbed at it with her handkerchief. "Oh, damn!" she muttered. The cloth was slowly becoming sodden. Suddenly her mouth twisted and her eyes were full of tears. She put her other hand over her face. "His first *real* chance. I'm so scared."

I didn't ask her *why*. I didn't want to hurry her. Instead, I asked, "What changed?"

Her shoulders knotted. But my question must've sounded safe to her. Gradually, some of her tension eased. "What do you mean?"

"He's been a sculptor for a long time." I did my best to sound reasonable, like a friend of her brother's. "But this is his first big show. What's different now? What's changed?"

The waiter ignored us, too bored to bother with customers who only wanted coffee. Numbly, Kristen took another handkerchief out of her purse, raised the fresh cloth to her nose. The other one went back into her purse. I already knew I was no friend of her brother's.

"He met a gallery owner." She sounded tired and sad. "Mortice Root. He calls his gallery The Root Cellar, but it's really an old brownstone mansion over on 49th. Reese went there to see him when the gallery first opened, two weeks ago. He said he was going to beg—. He's become so bitter. Most of the time, the people who run galleries won't even look at his work. I think he's been begging for years."

The idea made her defensive. "Failure does that to people. You work your heart out, but nothing in heaven or hell can force the people who control *access* to care about you. Gallery owners and agents can make or break you because they determine whether you get to show your work or not. You never even get to find out whether there's anything in your work that can touch or move or inspire people, no matter how hard you try, unless you can convince some owner he'll make a lot of money out of you."

But she was defending Reese from an accusation I hadn't made. Begging was easy to understand. Anybody who was hurt badly enough could do it. She was doing it herself—but she didn't realize it.

Or maybe she did. She drank some of her coffee and changed her tone. "But Mr. Root took him on," she said almost brightly. "He saw Reese's talent right away. He gave Reese a good contract and an advance. Reese has been working like a demon, getting ready—making new pieces. He's finally getting the chance he deserves."

The chance he deserves. I heard echoes in that—suggestions she hadn't intended. And she hadn't really answered my question. But I had another one now that was more important to me.

"Two weeks ago," I said. "Kristen, how long has your nose been bleeding?"

She stared at me while the enforced animation drained out of her face.

"Two weeks now, wouldn't you say?" I held her frightened eyes. "Off and on at first, so you didn't take it seriously? But now it's constant? If it weren't so slow, you'd choke yourself when you went to sleep at night?"

I'd gone too far. All at once, she stopped looking at me. She dropped her handkerchief, opened her purse, took out money and scattered it on the table. Then she covered her face again. "I've got to go," she said into her hand. "Reese hates being interrupted. But maybe there's something I can do to help him get ready for tomorrow."

She started to leave. And I stopped her. Just like that. Suddenly, she couldn't take herself away from me. A servant could sometimes wield the strength of his Lord.

I wanted to tell her she'd already given Reese more help than she could afford. But I didn't. I wasn't here to pronounce judgment. I didn't have that right. When I had her sitting in front of me again, I said, "You still haven't told me what changed."

Now she couldn't evade me—couldn't pretend she didn't understand. Slowly, she told me what had happened.

Mortice Root had liked Reese's talent—had praised it effusively—but he hadn't actually liked Reese's work. Too polite, he said. Too reasonable. Aesthetically perfect—emotionally boring. He urged Reese to "open up"—dig down into the energy of his fears and dreams, apply his great skill and talent to darker, more "honest" work. And he supplied Reese with new materials. Until then, Reese had worked in ordinary clay or wax, making castings of his figures only when he and Kristen were able to afford the caster's price. But Root had given Reese a special, black clay which gleamed like a river under a swollen moon. An ideal material, easy to work when it was damp, but finished when it dried, without need for firing or sealer or glaze—as hard and heavy as stone.

And as her brother's hands had worked that clay, Kristen's fear had grown out of it. His new pieces were indeed darker, images which chilled her heart. She used to love his work. Now she hated it.

I could've stopped then. I had enough to go on. And she wasn't the one I'd been sent to help; that was obvious. Maybe I should've stopped.

But I wanted to know more. That was my fault; I was forever trying to swim against the current. After all, the impulse to "open up"—to do darker, more "honest" work—was hardly evil. But the truth was, I was more interested in Kristen than Reese. Her eyes were full of supplication and abashment. She felt she had betrayed her brother, not so much by talking about him as by the simple fact that her attitude toward his work had changed. And she was still in such need—.

Instead of stopping, I took up another of the hints she hadn't given me. Quietly, I asked, "How long have you been supporting him?"

She was past being surprised now, but her eyes didn't leave my face. "Close to ten years," she answered obediently.

"That must've been hard on you."

"Oh, no," she said at once. "Not at all. I've been happy to do it." She was too loyal to say anything else. Here she was, with her life escaping from her—and she insisted she hadn't suffered. Her bravery made the backs of my eyes burn.

But I required honesty. After a while, the way I was looking at her made her say, "I don't really love my job. I work over in the garment district. I put in hems. After a few years"—she tried to sound self-deprecating and humorous—"it gets a little boring. And there's nobody I can talk to." Her tone suggested a deep gulf of loneliness. "But it's been worth it," she insisted. "I don't have any talent of my own. Supporting Reese gives me something to believe in. I make what he does possible."

I couldn't argue with that. She had made the whole situation possible. Grimly, I kept my mouth shut and waited for her to go on.

"The hard part," she admitted finally, "was watching him grow bitter." Tears started up in her eyes again, but she blinked them back. "All that failure—year after year—." She dropped her gaze; she couldn't bear to look at me and say such things. "He didn't have anybody else to take it out on."

That thought made me want to grind my teeth. She believed in him—and he took it out on her. She could've left him in any number of ways—gotten married, simply packed her bags, anything. But he probably wasn't even aware of the depth of her refusal to abandon him. He simply went on using her.

My own fear was gone now; I was too angry to be afraid. But I held it down. No matter how I felt, she wasn't the person I was here to defend. So I forced myself to sound positively casual as I said, "I'd like to meet him."

In spite of everything, she was still capable of being taken aback. "You want me to—?" She stared at me. "I couldn't!" She wasn't appalled; she was trying not to give in to a hope that must've seemed insane to her. "He hates being interrupted. He'd be furious." She scanned the table, hunting for excuses. "You haven't finished your coffee."

I nearly laughed out loud. I wasn't here for her—and yet she did wonderful things for me. Suddenly, I decided that it was all worth what it cost. Smiling broadly, I said, "I didn't say I needed coffee. I said you needed to buy it for me."

Involuntarily, the corners of her mouth quirked upward. Even with the handkerchief clutched to her face, she looked like a different person. After all she had endured, she was still a long way from being beaten. "Be serious," she said, trying to sound serious. "I can't take you home with me. I don't even know what to call you."

"If you take me with you," I responded, "you won't have to call me."

This time, I didn't need help to reach her. I just needed to go on smiling.

But what I was doing made sweat run down my spine. I didn't want to see her hurt any more. And there was nothing I could to to protect her.

The walk to the place where she and her brother lived seemed long and cruel in the heat. There were fewer cars and crowds around us now—most of the city's people had reached their destinations for the day—and thick, hot light glared at us from long aisles of pale concrete. At the same time, the buildings impacted on either side of us grew older, shabbier, became the homes of ordinary men and women rather than of money. Children played in the street, shrieking and running as if their souls were on fire. Derelicts shambled here and there, not so much lost to grace as inured by alcohol and ruin, benumbed by their own particular innocence. Several of the structures we passed had had their eyes blown out.

Then we arrived in front of a high, flat edifice indistinguishable from its surroundings except by the fact that most of its windows were intact. Kristen grimaced at it apologetically. "Actually," she said, "we could've been living better than this. But we save as much money as we can for Reese's work." She seemed to have forgotten that I looked worse than her apartment building did. Almost defiantly, she added, "Now we'll be able to do better."

That depended on what she called *better*. I was sure Mortice Root had no end of money. But I didn't say so.

However, she was still worried about how Reese would react to us. "Are you sure you want to do this?" she asked. "He isn't going to be on his good behavior."

I nodded and smiled; I didn't want her to see how scared and angry I was. "Don't worry about me. If he's rude, I can always offer him some constructive criticism."

"Oh, terrific," she responded, at once sarcastic and relieved, sourly amused. "He just *loves* constructive criticism."

She was hardly aware of her own bravery as she led me into the building.

The hall with the mail slots and the manager's apartment was dimly lit by one naked bulb; it should've felt cooler. But the heat inside was fierce. The stairs up to the fourth floor felt like a climb in a steambath. Maybe it was a blessing after all that I didn't have a shirt on under my coat. I was sweating so hard that my shoes felt slick and unreliable against my soles, as if every step I took was somehow untrustworthy.

When Kristen stopped at the door of her apartment, she needed both hands to fumble in her purse for the key. With her face uncovered, I saw that her nosebleed was getting worse.

Despite the way her hands shook, she got the door open. After finding a clean handkerchief, she ushered me inside, calling as she did so, "Reese! I'm home!"

The first room—it would've been the living room in anybody else's apartment—was larger than I'd expected; and it implied other rooms I couldn't see—bedrooms, a kitchen, a studio. The look of dinginess and unlove was part of the ancient wallpaper and warped baseboards, the sagging ceiling, not the result of carelessness; the place was scrupulously kempt. And the entire space was organized to display Reese's sculptures.

Set on packing crates and end tables, stacks of bricks, makeshift pedestals, old steamer trunks, they nearly filled the room. A fair number of them were cast; but most were clay, some fired, some not. And without exception they looked starkly out of place in that room. They were everything the apartment wasn't—finely done, idealistic, painless. It was as if Reese had left all his failure and bitterness and capacity for rage in the walls, sloughing it away from his work so that his art was kind and clean.

And static. It would've looked inert if he'd had less talent. Busts and madonnas stared with eyes that held neither fear nor hope. Children that never laughed or cried were hugged in the arms of blind women. A horse in one corner should've been prancing, but it was simply frozen. His bitterness he took out on his sister. His failures reduced him to begging. But his sculptures held no emotion at all.

They gave me an unexpected lift of hope. Not because they were static, but because he was capable of so much restraint. If reason was the circumference of energy, then he was already halfway to being a great artist. He had reason down pat.

Which was all the more surprising, because he was obviously not a reasonable man. He came bristling into the room in answer to Kristen's call, and he'd already started to shout at her before he saw I was there.

At once, he stopped; he stared at me. "Who the hell is *this?*" he rasped without looking at Kristen. I could feel the force of his intensity from where I stood. His face was as acute as a hawk's, whetted by the hunger and energy of a predator. But the dark stains of weariness and strain under his eyes made him look more feverish than fierce. All of a sudden I thought, Only two weeks to get a show ready. An entire show's worth of new pieces in only two weeks. Because of course he wasn't going to display any of the work I could see here. He was only going to show what he'd made out of the new, black clay Mortice Root had given him. And he'd worn himself ragged. In a sense, his intensity wasn't directed at me personally. It was just a fact of his personality. He did everything extremely. In his own way, he was as desperate as his sister. Maybe I should've felt sorry for him.

But he didn't give me much chance. Before I could say anything, he wheeled on Kristen. "It isn't bad enough you have to keep interrupting me," he snarled. "You have to bring trash in here too. Where did you find him—the Salvation Army? Haven't you figured out yet that I'm *busy?*"

I wanted to intervene; but she didn't need that kind of protection. Over her handkerchief, her eyes echoed a hint of her brother's fire. He took his bitterness out on her because she allowed him to, not because she was defenseless. Her voice held a bite of anger as she said, "He offered to help me."

If I hadn't been there, he might've listened to her. But his fever made him rash. "*Help* you?" he snapped. "This bum?" He looked at me again. "He couldn't help himself to another drink. And what do you need help—?"

"*Reese.*" This time, she got his attention. "I went to the doctor this morning."

"What?" For an instant, he blinked at her as if he couldn't understand. "The doctor?" The idea that something was wrong with her hit him hard. I could see his knees trying to fold under him. "You aren't sick. What do you need a doctor for?"

Deliberately, she lowered her hand, exposing the red sheen

darkening to crust on her upper lip, the blood swelling in her nostrils.

He gaped as if the sight nauseated him. Then he shook his head in denial. Abruptly, he sagged to the edge of a trunk that held two of his sculptures. "Damn it to hell," he breathed weakly. "Don't scare me like that. It's just a nosebleed. You've had it for weeks."

Kristen gave me a look of vindication; she seemed to think Reese had just shown how much he cared about her. But I wasn't so sure. I could think of plenty of selfish reasons for his reaction.

Either way, it was my turn to say something. I could've used some inspiration right then—just a little grace to help me find my way. My emotions were tangled up with Kristen; my attitude toward Reese was all wrong. I didn't know how to reach him. But no inspiration was provided.

Swallowing bile, I made an effort to sound confident. "Actually," I said, "I can be more help than you realize. That's the one advantage life has over art. There's more to it than meets the eye."

I was on the wrong track already; a halfwit could've done better. Reese raised his head to look at me, and the outrage in his eyes was as plain as a chisel. "That's wonderful," he said straight at me. "A bum *and* a critic."

Kristen's face was tight with dismay. She knew exactly what would happen if I kept going.

So did I. I wasn't stupid. But I was already sure I didn't really want to help Reese. I wanted somebody a little more worthy.

Anyway, I couldn't stop. His eyes were absolutely daring me to go on.

"Root's right," I said. Now I didn't have any trouble sounding as calm as a saint. "You know that. What you've been doing"— I gestured around the room—"is too controlled. Impersonal. You've got all the skill in the world, but you haven't put your heart into it.

"But I don't think he's been giving you very good advice. He's got you going to the opposite extreme. That's just another dead end. You need a balance. Control and passion. Control alone has been destroying you. Passion alone—"

Right there, I almost said it: passion alone will destroy your sister. That's the kind of bargain you're making. All it costs you is your soul.

But I didn't get the chance. Reese slapped his hand down on the trunk with a sound like a shot. One of his pieces tilted; it would've fallen if Kristen hadn't caught it. But he didn't see that. He jerked to his feet. Over his shoulder, he said to her, "You've been talking to this tramp about me." The words came out like lead.

She didn't answer. There was no defense against his accusation. To catch the sculpture, she'd had to use both hands. Her touch left a red smudge on the clay.

But he didn't seem to expect an answer. He was facing me with fever bright in his eyes. In the same heavy tone, he said, "It's your fault, isn't it. She wouldn't do that to me—tell a total stranger what a failure I've been—if you hadn't pried it out of her.

"Well, let me tell *you* something. Root owns a gallery. He has *power*." He spat the word as if he loathed it. "I have to listen to him. From you I don't have to take this kind of manure."

Which was true, of course. I was a fool—as well as being useless. But in simple chagrin I tried to stop or at least deflect what was coming.

"You're right," I said. "I've got no business trying to tell you what to do. But I can still help you. Just listen to me. I—"

"No," he retorted. "You listen. I've spent ten years of my life feeling the way you look. Now I've got a chance to do better. You don't know anything I could possibly want to hear. I've *been* there."

Still without looking at his sister, he said, "Kristen, tell him to leave."

She didn't have any choice. I'd botched everything past the point where there was anything she could do to save it. Reese would just rage at her if she refused—and what would that accomplish? I watched all the anger and hope drain out of her, and I wanted to fight back; but I didn't have any choice, either. She said in a beaten voice, "I think you'd better leave now," and I had to leave. I was no use to anybody without permission; I could not stay when she told me to go.

I didn't have the heart to squeeze in a last appeal on my way out. I didn't have any more hope than she did. I studied her face as I moved to the door, not because I thought she might change her mind, but because I wanted to memorize her, so that if she went on down this road and was lost in the end there would be at least one man left who remembered. But she didn't meet my eyes. And when I stepped out of the apartment, Reese slammed the door behind me so hard the floor shook.

The force of his rejection almost made me fall to my knees.

In spite of that, I didn't give up. I didn't know where I was or how I got here; I was lucky to know why I was here at all. And I would never remember. Where I was before I was here was as blank as a wall across the past. When the river took me someplace else, I wasn't going to be able to give Kristen Dona the bare courtesy of remembering her.

That was a blessing, of a sort. But it was also the reason I didn't give up. Since I didn't have any past or future, the present was my only chance.

When I was sure the world wasn't going to melt around me and change into something else, I went down the stairs, walked out into the pressure of the sun, and tried to think of some other way to fight for Kristen's life and Reese's soul.

After all, I had no right to give up hope on Reese. He'd been a failure for ten years. And I'd seen the way the people of this city looked at me. Even the derelicts had contempt in their eyes, including me in the way they despised themselves. I ought to be able to understand what humiliation could do to someone who tried harder than he knew how and still failed.

But I couldn't think of any way to fight it. Not without permission. Without permission, I couldn't even tell him his sister was in mortal danger.

The sun stayed nearly hidden behind its haze of humidity and dirt, but its brutality was increasing. Noon wasn't far away; the walk here had used up the middle of the morning. Heat waves shimmered off the pavement. An abandoned car with no wheels leaned against the curb like a cripple. Somebody had gone down the street and knocked over all the trashcans, scattering garbage like wasted lives. Somewhere there had to be something I could do to redeem myself. But when I prayed for help, I didn't get it.

After a while, I found myself staring as if I were about to go blind at a street sign at the corner of the block. A long time seemed to pass before I registered that the sign said, "21st St."

Kristen had said that Root's gallery, The Root Cellar, was "over on 49th."

I didn't know the city; but I could at least count. I went around the block and located 20th. Then I changed directions and started working my way up through the numbers.

It was a long hike. I passed through sections that were worse than where Kristen and Reese lived and ones that were better. I had a small scare when the numbers were interrupted, but after several blocks they took up where they'd left off. The sun kept leaning on me, trying to grind me into the pavement, and the air made my chest hurt.

And when I reached 49th, I didn't know which way to turn. Sweating, I stopped at the intersection and looked around. 49th seemed to stretch to the ends of the world in both directions. Anything was possible; The Root Cellar might be anywhere. I was in some kind of business district—49th was lined with prosperity—and the sidewalks were crowded again. But all the people moved as if nothing except fatigue or stubbornness and the heat kept them from running for their lives. I tried several times to stop one of them to ask directions; but it was like trying to change the course of the river. I got glares and muttered curses, but no help.

That was hard to forgive. But forgiveness wasn't my job. My job was to find some way to help Reese Dona. So I tried some outright begging. And when begging failed, I simply let the press of the crowds start me moving the same way they were going.

With my luck, this was exactly the wrong direction. But I couldn't think of any good reason to turn around, so I kept walking, studying the buildings for any sign of a brownstone mansion and muttering darkly against all those myths about how God answers prayer.

Ten blocks later, I recanted. I came to a store that filled the entire block and went up into the sky for at least thirty floors; and in front of it stood my answer. He was a scrawny old man in a dingy grey uniform with red epaulets and red stitching on his cap; boredom or patience glazed his eyes. He was tending an iron pot that hung from a rickety tripod. With the studious intention of a halfwit, he rang a handbell to attract people's attention.

The stitching on his cap said, "Salvation Army."

I went right up to him and asked where The Root Cellar was.

He blinked at me as if I were part of the heat and the haze. "Mission's that way." He nodded in the direction I was going. "49th and Grand."

"Thanks, anyway," I said. I was glad to be able to give the old man a genuine smile. "That isn't what I need. I need to find The Root Cellar. It's an art gallery. Supposed to be somewhere on 49th."

He went on blinking at me until I started to think maybe he was deaf. Then, abruptly, he seemed to arrive at some kind of recognition. Abandoning his post, he turned and entered the store. Through the glass, I watched him go to a box like half a booth that hung on one wall. He found a large yellow book under the box, opened it, and flipped the pages back and forth for a while.

Nodding at whatever he found, he came back out to me.

"Down that way," he said, indicating the direction I'd come from. "About thirty blocks. Number 840."

Suddenly, my heart lifted. I closed my eyes for a moment to give thanks. Then I looked again at the man who'd rescued me. "If I had any money," I said, "I'd give it to you."

"If you had any money," he replied, as if he knew who I was, "I wouldn't take it. Go with God."

I said, "I will," and started retracing my way up 49th.

I felt a world better. But I also had a growing sense of urgency. The longer I walked, the worse it got. The day was getting away from me—and this day was the only one I had. Reese's show was tomorrow. Then Mortice Root would've fulfilled his part of the bargain. And the price would have to be paid. I was sweating so hard my filthy old coat stuck to my back; but I forced myself to walk as fast as the fleeing crowds.

After a while, the people began to disappear from the sidewalks again and the traffic thinned. Then the business district came to an end, and I found myself in a slum so ruined and hopeless I had to grit my teeth to keep up my courage. I felt hostile eyes watching me from behind broken windows and gaping entrances. But I was protected, either by daylight or by the way I looked.

Then the neighborhood began to improve. The slum became close-built houses, clinging to dignity. The houses moved apart from each other, giving themselves more room to breathe. Trees appeared in the yards, even in the sidewalk. Lawns pushed the houses back from the street. And each house seemed to be more ornate than the one beside it. I would've thought they were homes, but most of them had discreet signs indicating they were places of business. Several of them were shops that sold antiques. One held a law firm. A stockbroker occupied a place the size of a temple. I decided that this was where people came to do their shopping and business when they were too rich to associate with their fellow human beings.

And there it was—a brownstone mansion as elaborate as any I'd seen. It was large and square, three stories tall, with a colonnaded entryway and a glass-domed structure that might have been a greenhouse down the length of one side. The mailbox on the front porch was neatly lettered, "840." And when I went up the walk to the porch, I saw a brass plaque on the door with words engraved on it. It said:

> The Root Cellar
> a private gallery
> Mortice Root

At the sight, my chest constricted as if I'd never done this before. But I'd already lost too much time; I didn't waste any more of it hesitating. I pressed a small button beside the door and listened to chimes ringing faintly inside the house as if Mortice Root had a cathedral in his basement.

For a while, nothing happened. Then the door opened, and I felt a flow of cold air from inside, followed by a man in a guard's uniform, with a gun holstered on his hip and a badge that said "Nationwide Security" on his chest. As he looked out at me, what he saw astonished him; not many of Root's patrons looked like I did. Then his face closed like a shutter. "Are you out of your mind?" he growled. "We don't give handouts here. Get lost."

In response, I produced my sweetest smile. "Fortunately, I don't want a handout. I want to talk to Mortice Root."

He stared at me. "What in hell makes you think Mr. Root wants to talk to you?"

"Ask him and find out," I replied. "Tell him I'm here to argue about Reese Dona."

He would've slammed the door in my face; but a hint of authority came back to me, and he couldn't do it. For a few moments, he gaped at me as if he were choking. Then he muttered, "Wait here," and escaped back into the house. As he closed the door, the cool air breathing outward was cut off.

"Well, naturally," I murmured to the sodden heat. Trying to keep myself on the bold side of dread. "The people who come here to spend their money can't be expected to just stand around and sweat."

The sound of voices came dimly through the door. But I hadn't heard the guard walk away, and I didn't hear anybody coming toward me. So I still wasn't quite ready when the door swung open again and Mortice Root stood in front of me with a cold breeze washing unnaturally past his shoulders.

We recognized each other right away; and he grinned like a wolf. But I couldn't match him. I was staggered. I hadn't expected him to be so *powerful*.

He didn't look powerful. He looked as rich as Solomon— smooth, substantial, glib—as if he could buy and sell the people who came here to give him their money. From the tips of his gleaming shoes past the expanse of his distinctively styled suit to the clean confidence of his shaven jowls, he was everything I wasn't. But those things only gave him worldly significance. They didn't make him powerful. His true strength was hidden behind the bland unction of his demeanor. It showed only in his grin, in the slight, avid bulging of his eyes, in the wisps of hair that stood out like hints of energy on either side of his bald crown.

His gaze made me feel grimy and rather pathetic.

He studied me for a moment. Then, with perfectly cruel kindness, he said, "Come in, come in. You must be sweltering out there. It's much nicer in here."

He was that sure of himself.

But I was willing to accept permission, even from him. Before he could reconsider, I stepped past him into the hallway.

Cold came swirling up my back, turning my sweat chill, as I looked around. At the end of this short, deeply carpeted hall, Root's mansion opened into an immense foyer nearly as high as the building itself. Two mezzanines joined by broad stairways of carved wood circled the walls; daylight shone downward from a skylight in the center of the ceiling. A glance showed me that paintings were displayed around the mezzanines, while the foyer itself held sculptures and carvings decorously set on white pedestals. I couldn't see anything that looked like Reese Dona's work.

At my elbow, Root said, "I believe you came to argue with me?" He was as smooth as oil.

I felt foolish and awkward beside him; but I faced him as squarely as I could. "Maybe 'contend' would be a better word."

"As you say." He chuckled in a way that somehow suggested both good humor and malice. "I look forward to it." Then he touched my arm, gestured me toward one side of the foyer. "But let me show you what he's doing these days. Perhaps you'll change your mind."

For no good reason, I said, "You know better than that." But I went with him.

A long, wide passage took us to the glass-domed structure I'd taken to be a greenhouse. Maybe it was originally built for that; but Root had converted it, and I had to admit it made an effective gallery—well-lit, spacious, and comfortable. In spite of all that glass, the air stayed cool, almost chill.

Here I saw Reese's new work for the first time.

"Impressive, aren't they," Root purred. He was mocking me.

But what he was doing to Reese was worse.

There were at least twenty of them, with room for a handful more—attractively set in niches along one wall, proudly positioned on special pediments, cunningly juxtaposed in corners so that they showed each other off. It was clear that any artist would find an opportunity like this hard to resist.

But all the pieces were black.

Reese had completely changed his subject matter. Madonnas and children had been replaced by gargoyles and twisted visions of the damned. Glimpses of nightmare leered from their niches. Pain writhed on display, as if it had become an object of ridicule. In a corner of the room, a ghoul devoured one infant while another strove urgently to scream and failed.

And each of these new images was alive with precisely the kind of vitality his earlier work lacked. He had captured his visceral terrors in the act of pouncing at him.

As sculptures, they were admirable; maybe even more than that. He had achieved some kind of breakthrough here, tapped into sources of energy he'd always been unable or unwilling to touch. All he needed now was balance.

But there was more to these pieces than just skill and energy. There was also blackness.

Root's clay.

Kristen was right. This clay looked like dark water under the light of an evil moon. It looked like marl mixed with blood until the mud congealed. And the more I studied what I saw, the more these grotesque and brutal images gave the impression of growing from the clay itself rather than from the independent mind of the artist. They were not Reese's fears and dreams refined by art; they were horrors he found in the clay when his hands touched it. The real strength, the passion of these pieces, came from the material Root supplied, not from Reese. No wonder he had become so hollow-eyed and ragged. He was struggling desperately to control the consequences of his bargain. Trying to prove to himself he wasn't doing the wrong thing.

For a moment, I felt a touch of genuine pity for him.

But it didn't last. Maybe deep down in his soul he was afraid of what he was doing and what it meant. But he was still doing it. And he was paying for the chance to do such strong work with his sister's life.

Softly, my opponent said, "It appears you don't approve. I'm so sorry. But I'm afraid there's really nothing you can do about it. The artists of this world are uniquely vulnerable. They wish to create beauty, and the world cares for nothing but money. Even the cattle who will buy these"—he gave the room a dismissive flick of the hand—"trivial pieces hold the artist in contempt." He turned his wolf grin toward me again. "Failure makes fertile ground."

I couldn't pretend that wasn't true; so I asked bitterly, "Are you really going to keep your end of the bargain? Are you really going to sell this stuff?"

"Oh, assuredly," he replied. "At least until the sister dies. Tomorrow. Perhaps the day after." He chuckled happily. "Then I suspect I'll find myself too busy with other, more promising artists to spend time on Reese Dona."

I felt him glance at me, gauging my helplessness. Then he went on unctuously, "Come, now, my friend. Why glare so thunderously? Surely you realize that he has been using her in precisely this manner for years. I've merely actualized the true state of their relationship. But perhaps you're too innocent to grasp how deeply he resents her. It is the nature of beggars to resent those who give them gifts. He resents *me*." At that, Root laughed outright. He was not a man who gave gifts to anybody. "I assure you that her present plight is of his own choice and making."

"No," I said, more out of stubbornness than conviction. "He just doesn't understand what's happening."

Root shrugged. "Do you think so? No matter. The point, as you must recognize, is that we have nothing to contend *for*. The issue has already been decided."

I didn't say anything. I wasn't as glib as he was. And anyway, I was afraid he was right.

While I stood there and chewed over all the things I wasn't able to do, I heard doors opening and closing somewhere in the distance. The heavy carpeting absorbed footsteps; but it wasn't long before Reese came striding into the greenhouse. He was so tight with eagerness or suppressed fear he looked like he was about to snap. As usual, he didn't even see me when he first came into the room.

"I've got the rest of the pieces," he said to Root. "They're in a truck out back. I think you'll like—"

Then my presence registered on him. He stopped with a jerk, stared at me as if I'd come back from the dead. "What're *you* doing here?" he demanded. At once, he turned back to Root. "What is *he* doing here?"

Root's confidence was a complete insult. "Reese," he sighed, "I'm afraid that this—gentleman?—believes that I should not show your work tomorrow."

For a moment, Reese was too astonished to be angry. His mouth actually hung open while he looked at me. But I was furious enough for both of us. With one sentence, Root had made my position impossible. I couldn't think of a single thing to say now that would change the outcome.

Still, I had to try. While Reese's surprise built up into outrage, I said, as if I weren't swearing like a madman inside, "There are two sides to everything. You've heard his. You really ought to listen to mine."

He closed his mouth, locked his teeth together. His glare was wild enough to hurt.

"Mortice Root owes you a little honesty," I said while I had the chance. "He should've told you long ago that he's planning to drop you after tomorrow."

But the sheer pettiness of what I was saying made me cringe. And Root simply laughed. I should've known better than to try to fight him on his own level. Now he didn't need to answer me at all.

In any case, my jibe made no impression on Reese. He gritted, "I don't care about that," like a man who couldn't or wouldn't understand. "This is what I care about." He gestured frantically around the room. "*This*. My work."

He took a couple steps toward me, and his voice shook with the effort he made to keep from shouting. "I don't know who you are—or why you think I'm any of your business. I don't care about that, either. You've heard Kristen's side. Now you're going to hear mine."

In a small way, I was grateful he didn't accuse me of turning his sister against him.

"She doesn't like the work I'm doing now. No, worse than that. She doesn't mind the work. She doesn't like the *clay*." He gave a laugh like an echo of Root's. But he didn't have Root's confidence and power; he only sounded bitter, sarcastic, and afraid. "She tries to tell me she approves of me, but I can read her face like a book.

"Well, let me tell you something." He poked a trembling finger at my chest. "With my show tomorrow, I'm alive for the first time in ten years. I'm alive *here*. Art exists to communicate. It isn't worth manure if it doesn't communicate. And it can't communicate if somebody doesn't look at it. It's that simple. The only time an artist is alive is when somebody looks at his work. And if enough people look, he can live forever.

"I've been sterile for ten years because I haven't had one other soul to look at my work." He was so wrapped up in what he was saying, I don't think he even noticed how completely he dismissed his sister. "Now I am alive. If it only lasts for one more day, it'll still be something nobody can take away from me. If I have to work in black clay to get that, who cares? That's just something I didn't know about myself—about how my imagination works. I never had the chance to try black clay before.

"But now—." He couldn't keep his voice from rising like a cry. "Now I'm alive. *Here*. If you want to take that away from me, you're worse than trash. You're evil."

Mortice Root was smiling like a saint.

For a moment, I had to look away. The fear behind the passion in Reese's eyes was more than I could stand. "I'm sorry," I murmured. What else could I say? I regretted everything. He needed me desperately, and I kept failing him. And he placed so little value on his sister. With a private groan, I forced myself to face him again.

"I thought it was work that brought artists to life. Not shows. I thought the work was worth doing whether anybody looked at it or not. Why else did you keep at it for ten years?"

But I was still making the same mistake, still trying to reach him through his art. And now I'd definitely said something he couldn't afford to hear or understand. With a jerky movement like a puppet, he threw up his hands. "I don't have time for this," he snapped. "I've got five more pieces to set up." Then, suddenly, he was yelling at me. "And I don't give one lousy damn what you think!" Somehow, I'd hit a nerve. "I want you to go away. I want you to leave me alone! Get out of here and *leave me alone!*"

I didn't have any choice. As soon as he told me to go, I turned toward the door. But I was desperate myself now. Knotting my fists, I held myself where I was. Urgently—so urgently that I could hardly separate the words—I breathed at him, "Have you looked at Kristen recently? Really looked? Haven't you seen what's happening to her? You—"

Root stopped me. He had that power. Reese had told me to go. Root simply raised his hand, and his strength hit me in the chest like a fist. My tongue was clamped to the roof of my mouth. My voice choked in my throat. For one moment while I staggered, the greenhouse turned in a complete circle, and I thought I was going to be thrown out of the world.

But I wasn't. A couple of heart-beats later, I got my balance back.

Helpless to do anything else, I left the greenhouse.

As I crossed the foyer toward the front door, Reese shouted after me, "And stay away from my sister!"

Until I closed the door, I could hear Mortice Root chuckling with pleasure.

Dear God! I prayed. Let me decide. Just this once. He isn't worth it.

But I didn't have the right.

On the other hand, I didn't have to stay away from Kristen. That was up to her; Reese didn't have any say in the matter.

I made myself walk slowly until I was out of sight of The Root Cellar, just in case someone was watching. Then I started to run.

It was the middle of the afternoon, and the heat just kept getting worse. After the cool of Root's mansion, the outside air felt like glue against my face. Sweat oozed into my eyes, stuck my coat to my back, itched maliciously in my dirty whiskers. The sunlight looked like it was congealing on the walks and streets. Grimly I thought, If this city doesn't get some rain soon it will start to burn.

And yet I wanted the day to last, despite the heat. I would happily have caused the sun to stand still. I did not want to have to face Mortice Root and Reese Dona again after dark.

But I would have to deal with that possibility when it came up. First I had to get Kristen's help. And to do that, I had to reach her.

The city did its best to hinder me. I left Root's neighborhood easily enough; but when I entered the slums, I started having problems. I guess a running man dressed in nothing but an overcoat, a pair of pants, and sidesplit shoes looked like too much fun to miss. Gangs of kids seemed to materialize out of the ruined buildings to get in my way.

They should've known better. They were predators themselves, and I was on hunt of my own; when they saw the danger in my eyes, they backed down. Some of them threw bottles and trash at my back, but that didn't matter.

Then the sidewalks became more and more crowded as the slum faded behind me. People stepped in front of me, jostled me off my stride, swore angrily at me as I tried to run past. I had to slow down just to keep myself out of trouble. And all the lights were against me. At every corner, I had to wait and wait while mobs hemmed me in, instinctively blocking the path of anyone who wanted to get ahead of them. I felt like I was up against an active enemy. The city was rising to defend its own.

By the time I reached the street I needed to take me over to 21st, I felt so ragged and wild I wanted to shake my fists at the sky and demand some kind of assistance or relief. But if God couldn't see how much trouble I was in, He didn't deserve what

I was trying to do in His name. So I did the best I could—running in spurts, walking when I had to, risking the streets whenever I saw a break in the traffic. And finally I made it. Trembling, I reached the building where Reese and Kristen had their apartment.

Inside, it was as hot as an oven, baking its inhabitants to death. But here at least there was nobody in my way, and I took the stairs two and three at a time to the fourth floor. The lightbulb over the landing was out, but I didn't have any trouble finding the door I needed.

I pounded on it with my fist. Pounded again. Didn't hear anything. Hammered at the wood a third time.

"Kristen!" I shouted. I didn't care how frantic I sounded. "Let me in! I've got to talk to you!"

Then I heard a small, faint noise through the panels. She must've been right on the other side of the door. Weakly, she said, "Go away."

"Kristen!" Her dismissal left a welt of panic across my heart. I put my mouth to the crack of the door to make her hear me. "Reese needs help. If he doesn't get it, you're not going to survive. He doesn't even realize he's sacrificing you."

After a moment, the lock clicked, and the door opened.

I went in.

But the apartment was dark. She'd turned off all the lights. When she closed the door behind me, I couldn't see a thing. I had to stand still so I wouldn't bump into Reese's sculptures.

"Kristen," I said, half pleading, half commanding. "Turn on a light."

Her reply was a whisper of misery. "You don't want to see me."

She sounded so beaten I almost gave up hope. Quietly, I said, "Please."

She couldn't refuse. She needed me too badly. I felt her move past me in the dark. Then the overhead lights clicked on, and I saw her.

I shouldn't have been shocked. I knew what to expect. But that didn't help. The sight of her went into me like a knife.

She was wearing only a terrycloth bathrobe. That made sense; she'd been poor for a long time and didn't want to ruin her good clothes. The collar of her robe was soaked with blood.

Her nosebleed was worse.

And delicate red streams ran steadily from both her ears.

Sticky trails marked her lips and chin, the front of her throat, the sides of her neck. She'd given up trying to keep herself clean. Why should she bother? She was bleeding to death, and she knew it.

Involuntarily, I went to her and put my arms around her.

She leaned against me. I was all she had left. Into my shoulder, she said as if she were on the verge of tears, "I can't help him anymore. I've tried and tried. I don't know what else to do."

She stood there quivering; and I held her and stroked her hair and let her blood soak into my coat. I didn't have any other way to comfort her.

But her time was running out, just like Reese's. The longer I waited, the weaker she would be. As soon as she became a little steadier, I lowered my arms and stepped back. In spite of the way I looked, I wanted her to be able to see what I was.

"He doesn't need that kind of help now," I said softly, willing her to believe me. "Not the kind you've been giving him for ten years. Not anymore. He needs me. That's why I'm here.

"But I have to have permission." I wanted to cry at her, You've been letting him do this to you for ten years! None of this would've happened to you if you hadn't allowed it! But I kept that protest to myself. "He keeps sending me away, and I have to go. I don't have any choice. I can't do anything without permission.

"It's really that simple." God, make her believe me! "I need somebody with me who wants me to be there. I need you to go back to The Root Cellar with me. Even Root won't be able to get rid of me if you want me to stay.

"Kristen." I moved closer to her again, put my hands in the blood on her cheek, on the side of her neck. "I'll find some way to save him. If you're there to give me permission."

She didn't look at me; she didn't seem to have the courage to raise her eyes. But after a moment I felt the clear touch of grace. She believed me—when I didn't have any particular reason to believe myself. Softly, she said, "I can't go like this. Give me a minute to change my clothes."

She still didn't look at me. But when she turned to leave the room, I saw determination mustering in the corners of her eyes.

I breathed a prayer of long overdue thanks. She intended to fight.

I waited for her with fear beating in my bones. And when she returned—dressed in her dingy blouse and fraying skirt, with a towel wrapped around her neck to catch the blood—and announced that she was ready to go, I faltered. She looked so wan and frail—already weak and unnaturally pale from loss of blood. I felt sure she wasn't going to be able to walk all the way to The Root Cellar.

Carefully, I asked her if there was any other way we could get where we were going. But she shrugged the question aside. She and Reese had never owned a car. And he'd taken what little money was available in order to rent a truck to take his last pieces to the gallery.

Groaning a silent appeal for help, I held her arm to give her what support I could. Together, we left the apartment, went down the old stairs and out to the street.

I felt a new sting of dread when I saw that the sun was setting. For all my efforts to hurry, I'd taken too much time. Now I would have to contend with Mortice Root at night.

Twilight and darkness brought no relief from the heat. The city had spent all day absorbing the pressure of the sun; now the walks and buildings, every stretch of cement seemed to emit fire like the sides of a furnace. The air felt thick and ominous—as charged with intention as a thunderstorm, but trapped somehow, prevented from release, tense with suffering.

It sucked the strength out of Kristen with every breath. Before we'd gone five blocks, she was bracing most of her weight on me. That was frightening, not because she was more than I could bear, but because she seemed to weigh so little. Her substance was bleeding away. In the garish and unreliable light of the street-lamps, show windows, and signs, only the dark marks on her face and neck appeared real.

But we were given one blessing: the city itself left us alone. It had done its part by delaying me earlier. We passed through crowds and traffic, past gutted tenements and stalking gangs, as if we didn't deserve to be noticed anymore.

Kristen didn't complain, and I didn't let her stumble. One by one, we covered the blocks. When she wanted to rest, we put our backs to the hot walls and leaned against them until she was ready to go on.

During that whole long, slow creep through the pitiless dark, she only spoke to me once. While we were resting again, some-time after we turned on 49th, she said quietly, "I still don't know your name."

We were committed to each other; I owed her the truth. "I don't either," I said. Behind the wall of the past, any number of things were hidden from me.

She seemed to accept that. Or maybe she just didn't have enough strength left to worry about both Reese and me. She rested a little while longer. Then we started walking again.

And at last we left the last slum behind and made our slow, frail approach to The Root Cellar. Between streetlights I looked for the moon, but it wasn't able to show through the clenched haze. I was sweating like a frightened animal. But Kristen might have been immune to the heat. All she did was lean on me and walk and bleed.

I didn't know what to expect at Root's mansion. Trouble of some kind. An entire squadron of security guards. Minor demons lurking in the bushes around the front porch. Or an empty build-ing, deserted for the night. But the place wasn't deserted. All the rest of the mansion was dark; the greenhouse burned with light. Reese wasn't able to leave his pieces alone before his show. And none of the agents that Root might have used against us appeared. He was that sure of himself.

On the other hand, the front door was locked with a variety of bolts and wires.

But Kristen was breathing sharply, urgently. Fear and desire and determination made her as feverish as her brother; she wanted me to take her inside, to Reese's defense. And she'd lost a dangerous amount of blood. She wasn't going to be able to stay on her feet much longer. I took hold of the door, and it opened without a sound. Cool air poured out at us, as concentrated as a moan of anguish.

We went in.

The foyer was dark. But a wash of light from the cracks of the greenhouse doors showed us our way. The carpet muffled our feet. Except for her ragged breathing and my frightened heart, we were as silent as spirits.

But as we got near the greenhouse, I couldn't keep quiet anymore. I was too scared.

I caused the doors to burst open with a crash that shook the walls. At the same time, I tried to charge forward.

The brilliance of the gallery seemed to explode in my face. For an instant, I was dazzled.

And I was stopped. The light felt as solid as the wall that cut me off from the past.

Almost at once, my vision cleared, and I saw Mortice Root and Reese Dona. They were alone in the room. They were standing in front of a sculpture I hadn't seen earlier—the biggest piece here. Reese must've brought it in his rented truck. It was a wild, swept-winged, and malignant bird of prey, its beak wide in a cry of fury. One of its clawed feet was curled like a fist. The other was gripped deep into a man's chest. Agony stretched the man's face.

At least Reese had the decency to be surprised. Root wasn't. He faced us and grinned.

Reese gaped dismay at Kristen and me for one moment. Then,

with a wrench like an act of violence, he turned his back. His shoulders hunched; his arms clamped over his stomach. "I told you to go away." His voice sounded like he was strangling. "I told you to leave her alone."

The light seemed to blow against me like a wind. Like the current of the river that carried me away, taking me from place to place without past and without future hope. And it was rising. It held me in the doorway; I couldn't move through it.

"You are a fool," Root said to me. His voice rode the light as if he were shouting. "You have been denied. You cannot enter here."

He was so strong that I was already half turned to leave when Kristen saved me.

As pale as ash, she stood beside me. Fresh blood from her nose and ears marked her skin. The towel around her neck was sodden and terrible. She looked too weak to keep standing. Yet she matched her capacity for desperation against Reese's need.

"No," she said in the teeth of the light and Root's grin. "He can stay. I want him here."

I jerked myself toward Reese again.

Ferocity came at me like a cataract; but I stood against it. I had Kristen's permission. That had to be enough.

"Look at her!" I croaked at his back. "She's your sister! *Look* at her!"

He didn't seem to hear me at all. He was hunched over himself in front of his work. "Go away," he breathed weakly, as if he were talking to himself. "I can't stand it. Just go away."

Gritting prayers between my teeth like curses, I lowered my head, called up every ache and fragment of strength I had left, and took one step into the greenhouse.

Reese fell to his knees as if I'd broken the only string that held him upright.

At the same time, the bird of prey poised above him moved.

Its wings beat downward. Its talons clenched. The heart of its victim burst in his chest.

From his clay throat came a brief, hoarse wail of pain.

Driven by urgency, I took two more steps through the intense pressure walled against me.

And all the pieces displayed in the greenhouse started to move.

Tormented statuettes fell from their niches, cracked open, and cried out. Gargoyles mewed hideously. The mouths of victims gaped open and whined. In a few swift moments, the air was full of muffled shrieks and screams.

Through the pain, and the fierce current forcing me away from Reese, and the horror, I heard Mortice Root start to laugh.

If Kristen had failed me then, I would have been finished. But in some way she had made herself blind and deaf to what was happening. Her entire soul was focused on one object—help for her brother—and she willed me forward with all the passion she had learned in ten years of self-sacrifice. She was prepared to spend her last life here for Reese's sake.

She made it possible for me to keep going.

Black anguish rose like a current at me. And the force of the light mounted. I felt it ripping at my skin. It was as hot as the hunger ravening for Reese's heart.

Yet I took two more steps.

And two more.

And reached him.

He still knelt under the wingspread of the nightmare bird he had created. The light didn't hurt him; he didn't feel it at all. He was on his knees because he simply couldn't stand. He gripped his arms over his heart to keep himself from howling.

Then I noticed something I should've recognized earlier. He had sculpted a man for his bird of prey to attack, not a woman. I could see the figure clearly enough now to realize that Reese had given the man his own features. Here, at least, he had shaped one of his own terrors rather than merely bringing out the darkness of Mortice Root's clay.

After that, nothing else mattered. I didn't feel the pain or the pressure. Ferocity and dismay lost their power.

I knelt in front of Reese, took hold of his shoulders, and hugged him like a child. "Just look at her," I breathed into his ear. "She's your sister. You don't have to do this to her."

She stood across the room from me with her eyes closed and her determination gripped in her small fists.

From under her eyelids, stark blood streamed down her cheeks. "Look at her!" I pleaded. "I can help you. Just *look*."

In the end, he didn't look at her. He didn't need to. He knew what was happening.

Suddenly, he wrenched out of my embrace. His arms flung me aside. He raised his head, and one lorn wail corded his throat:

"*Kristen!*"

Root's laughter stopped as if it'd been cut down with an axe.

That cry was all I needed. It came right from Reese's heart, too pure to be denied. It was permission, and I took it.

I rose to my feet, easily now, easily. All the things that stood in my way made no difference. Transformed, I faced Mortice Root across the swelling force of his malice. All his confidence was gone to panic.

Slowly, I raised my arms.

Beams of white sprouted from my palms, clean white, almost silver. It wasn't fire or light in any worldly sense; but it blazed over my head like light, ran down my arms like fire. It took my coat and pants, even my shoes, away from me in flames. Then it wrapped me in the robes of God until all my body burned.

Root tried to scream, but his voice didn't make any sound.

Towering white-silver, I reached up into the storm-dammed sky and brought down a blast that staggered the entire mansion to its foundations. Crashing past glass and frame and light fixtures, a bolt that might have been lightning took hold of Root from head to foot. For an instant, the gallery's lights failed. Everything turned black except for Root's horror etched against darkness and the blast that bore him away.

When the lights came back on, the danger was gone from the greenhouse. All the crying and the pain and the pressure were gone. Only the sculptures themselves remained.

They were slumped and ruined, like melted wax.

Outside, rain began to rattle against the glass of the greenhouse.

Later, I went looking for some clothes; I couldn't very well go around naked. After a while, I located a suite of private rooms at the back of the building. But everything I found there belonged to Root. His personal stink had soaked right into the fabric. I hated the idea of putting his things on my skin when I'd just been burned clean. But I had to wear something. In disgust, I took one of his rich shirts and a pair of pants. That was my punishment for having been so eager to judge Reese Dona.

Back in the greenhouse, I found him sitting on the floor with Kristen's head cradled in his lap. He was stroking the soft hair at her temples and grieving to himself. For the time being, at least, I was sure his grief had nothing to do with his ruined work.

Kristen was fast asleep, exhausted by exertion and loss of blood. But I could see that she was going to be all right. Her bleeding had stopped completely. And Reese had already cleaned some of the stains from her face and neck.

Rain thundered against the ceiling of the greenhouse; jagged lines of lightning scrawled the heavens. But all the glass was intact, and the storm stayed outside, where it belonged. From the safety of shelter, the downpour felt comforting.

And the manufactured cool of the building had wiped out most of Root's unnatural heat. That was comforting, too.

It was time for me to go.

But I didn't want to leave Reese like this. I couldn't do anything about the regret that was going to dog him for the rest of his life. But I wanted to try.

The river was calling for me. Abruptly, as if I thought he was in any shape to hear me, I said, "What you did here—the work you did for Root—wasn't wrong. Don't blame yourself for that. You just went too far. You need to find the balance. Reason and energy." Need and help. "There's no limit to what you can do, if you just keep your balance."

He didn't answer. Maybe he wasn't listening to me at all. But after a moment he bent over Kristen and kissed her forehead.

That was enough. I had to go. Some of the details of the greenhouse were already starting to melt.

My bare feet didn't make any sound as I left the room, crossed the foyer, and went out into—

· About the Authors ·

HILARY ANDREWES has been writing since she was very young, although "Someone to Watch Over Me" is her first published story. She is the only child of two inveterate readers and grew up on and around college campuses along the eastern seaboard. Her childhood was, in her words, "perfectly ordinary, filled with friends and birthday parties and the occasional summer camp—certainly not the stuff of high drama!"

Miss Andrewes has been married for eight years to a man who shares her love of reading. They live near the ocean and maintain that they would not want to stay for long anywhere else. "The ocean inspires me and comforts me and uplifts me," Miss Andrewes says. "I find the vastness of it and the constant sound of the waves very soothing. I never sleep as well as I do when I am surrounded by the sounds of the gulls and the fog horns."

After her graduation from college in the mid-seventies, she held a variety of jobs, but her first love has always been writing, and even when she was working days in other fields, she frequently spent nights at the typewriter. At the moment she is at work on a full-length fantasy and someday would like to return to Polyhistor and Kate, developing this story into a longer format. In the meantime, when she isn't writing, Miss Andrewes enjoys gardening and photography. "I am just learning about photography," she writes, "but I find it fascinating—much like writing. You take something that is three-dimensional, put it in a two-dimensional form, and give it to someone who will use his imagination to turn it back into three dimensions. And it isn't the same when it has gone through that process. An idea changes when it is put into words, it takes on a life of its own; the same thing happens when a scene is put onto photographic paper. People who read the story or look at the picture bring all their background and dreams and thoughts with them. I think that is one of the things I love most about art: it is shared. It isn't only the artist who works on a piece—everyone who sees it helps."

STEPHEN DONALDSON was born in 1947 in Cleveland, Ohio. He spent a large part of his childhood in India, where his father—known for his pioneering work on tuberculosis of the spine—was an orthopedic surgeon serving as a medical missionary. Mr. Donaldson returned to the United States and took his B.A. in English Literature at the College of Wooster in 1968 and his M.A.—also in English Literature—at Kent State University in 1971.

Since college he has devoted himself to writing, and in 1977 "The Chronicles of Thomas Covenant the Unbeliever" were published by Holt, Rinehart & Winston. "The Chronicles" included *Lord Foul's Bane*, *The Illearth War*, and *The Power That Preserves*. Critical and popular acclaim followed, and in 1979 Mr. Donaldson was awarded both the British Fantasy Society Award for Best Novel and the coveted John W. Campbell Award for Best New Writer. In 1980, "The Second Chronicles of Thomas Covenant" began with *The Wounded Land*, which promptly won the Balrog Fantasy Award for Best Novel in 1981. The fifth book, *The One Tree*, was published in 1982 and moved quickly onto the *New York Times* Best Seller List. It was followed in 1983 by the sixth, *White Gold Wielder*.

Meanwhile, Mr. Donaldson has published one novel under the pseudonym Reed Stephens (*The Man Who Killed His Brother*), and has written and published several short stories, including "The Lady in White" and "Mythological Beast."

Stephen Donaldson lives with his wife, Stephanie Boutz, in a small village in New Mexico where "the desert—like the mountains—is never far away." In fact, as he goes on to say, "I have an acre of it in my backyard." For pleasure, he plays an avid but erratic game of bridge.

Donaldson has strong views on writing and on fantasy: "I consider fiction to be the only valid tool for theological inquiry. And I consider fantasy to be the most human and fundamental form of fiction. So it follows that I consider all really good fantasy to be religious fantasy on one level or another."

JOANNE GREENBERG has lived for twenty years in Colorado with her husband Albert, a retired vocational rehabilitation counselor. Their two sons, David and Alan, grew up among the mountains and are now busy with their own careers. Miss Greenberg was born in Brooklyn, New York, and studied at both the University of Colorado and the University of London before taking her B.A. from American University in 1955.

In the years since graduation, she has devoted herself to writing, for which she has won such awards as the Daroff Memorial Award for Fiction in 1963, the Fromm Reichmann Award in 1967 and both the Kenner and Christopher Awards in 1971. She has also been awarded two honorary doctorates, one in 1977 from Western Maryland College and the second in 1979 from Gallaudet.

Her books of fiction include *The King's Person, The Monday Voices, Founder's Praise,* and *A Season of Delight.* Her short stories are to be found in *Summering, Rites of Passages* and *High Crimes and Misdemeanors.* "Certain Distant Suns" first appeared in the last-named in 1979. Undoubtedly her best-known work is the novel *I Never Promised You a Rose Garden,* written under the pseudonym of Hannah Green.

In addition to being a member of such professional organizations as the Authors' Guild, the Colorado Authors' League, and P.E.N., Miss Greenberg is also involved in the National Assocation for the Deaf, the Lookout Mountain Fire Department, and the Ladies' Tuesday Skiing and Terrorist Society.

She writes, "I think fantasy is like a jet which will take you as high and as fast as you want to go, but you have to start on the earth and end on the earth . . . that is to say that you have to start with reality and end with reality."

ROBERT DON HUGHES was born in 1949 and is the product of what he calls "a Southern heritage and a California upbringing." His undergraduate studies were in drama, which he followed with two years in Zambia. He returned to the United States to complete his schooling with a Master of Divinity and a Doctor of Philosophy in Christian Missions, World Religions, and Christian Philosophy. After some particularly joyous time spent as the pastor of a small rural church in Kentucky, he moved with his wife, Gail, and three-year-old daughter,

Bronwynn, to Nigeria, where he was a missionary in charge of mass media ministry for the Baptists. He is now back in this country as pastor of a church in rural Alabama.

His previous writings include *The Prophet of Lamath* and *The Wizard in Waiting* (both published by Del Rey), which have as their protagonist Pelmen, the central figure in "Pursuit of a Lost Tugolith." The third book in the Pelmen series came out in 1983. Dr. Hughes has also written and had published several plays, including "Mountaintop," "With Bonds of Love," "The Upper Room," and "The Stone Congregation."

He explains his philosophy: "I write fantasy for the same reason I read it—escape. But I also find it a good genre for putting ideas forward, especially Christian ideas that are (to me) eternally true, but begin to sound boring when encrusted in theological language. In fantasy, the images aren't frozen in layers of interpretive material."

KATHERINE KURTZ was born in 1941 in Coral Gables, Florida, in the middle of a hurricane. In spite of the weather, her family seems to have liked Florida, for she grew up there and eventually graduated from the University of Miami with a B.S. in chemistry. She then went west to the Los Angeles area and took her M.A. in medieval English history from UCLA. She has drawn heavily from these studies for the background of her two trilogies: *The Chronicles of the Deryni* and *The Legends of Camber of Culdi*, both published by Ballantine Books, the latter under the Del Rey label.

The first book of the Camber trilogy, *Camber of Culdi*, received the Edmond Hamilton Memorial Award in 1977; the second, *Saint Camber*, was nominated in 1978 for the Gandalf Award for best book-length fantasy; the third, *Camber the Heretic*, received the prestigious Balrog Award in 1982. In and around the two complete trilogies, Miss Kurtz has found time to write several short stories, including "Healer's Song," "Legacy," "Bethane," and "Swords Against Marluk." She has also finished a non-Deryni novel set in World War II, called *The Lammas Option*, which was published in 1983.

In addition to a full life as a writer, Miss Kurtz is a member of the Society for Creative Anachronism and the Augustan Society (a heraldic and genealogical organization), as well as belonging to the Science

Fiction Writers of America. She enjoys working with her hands at such diverse skills as counted cross-stitch, needlepoint, sewing, calligraphy, and woodworking. When she needs a break from sitting still, she can be found riding her bay quarterhorse, Jubal; Regency dancing; or travel-ing—Great Britain is, understandably, a favorite destination.

Miss Kurtz has this to say about "Vocation": " . . . [this] story just sprang full-blown into being. I intend to fill in a great deal of time between Camber and Kelson, and it seemed that this was a story that needed to be told. I'm hoping to do at least a novella from the back-ground I've woven here."

Looking into the future, she is currently at work on *The Young Kelson Trilogy*, following chronologically on *The Chronicles of the Deryni*, the first of these appearing in 1983. At least two more Deryni trilogies are projected after that.

MADELEINE L'ENGLE describes herself as a "myopic giraffe," and the image is not inaccurate. She moves nearsightedly and with a stately grace through the most hectic of days. When she needs to move quickly, she lopes. In and around a schedule that would exhaust most cam-paigning politicians, she has found time to write over thirty books (poetry, novels, non-fiction, and two plays). As she is fond of telling the young readers who flood her with mail, she "simply started writing stories at age five, and never stopped." Much of her early childhood was spent in Anglican boarding schools; she finished her formal edu-cation at Smith College, from which she graduated with honors in 1941. She has continued to learn, however. Her reading in the fields of higher mathematics and astrophysics, as well as about advances in medicine, the mysteries of black holes, and the discovery of the history of the Welsh community in Patagonia, provided the plots for some of her best-known works, the three books which comprise "The Time Trilogy": *A Wrinkle in Time* (which won the Newberry Medal in 1962), *A Wind in the Door*, and *A Swiftly Tilting Planet* (which was honored with The American Book Award in 1978).

Miss L'Engle met her husband, the actor Hugh Franklin, while work-ing as an actress. As she puts it, "We met in 'The Cherry Orchard' and married in 'The Joyous Season.'" They are the parents of three children and spent ten years as shopkeepers of a general store while the children were young. They now live in a rambling apartment in Manhattan and an old house, "Crosswicks," in Connecticut.

As her writing has become more widely known, she has spent an increasing amount of time traveling and speaking to writers' conferences, students, college English professors, and, lately, church groups. In the past decade, she has begun to lead retreats, an avocation which has enriched both her life and her writing. In 1978 she distilled some of her retreat meditations into *Walking on Water*, which articulates many of her ideas concerning the vocation and responsibilities of the creative artist.

With her children now established in their own careers and marriages, Miss L'Engle lives with an Irish setter named Timothy and her husband, who plays Dr. Tyler on the television series "All My Children". Crosswicks is the setting for "The Crosswicks Journal," the three books of which—*A Circle of Quiet, The Summer of the Great-Grandmother, The Irrational Season*—are published by The Seabury Press.

Miss L'Engle is a member of the Board of Governors of The American Society of The Most Venerable Order of The Hospital of St. John of Jerusalem, the order of which Her Majesty, Queen Elizabeth II, is the Sovereign Head. Her papers are in the famous collection at Wheaton College.

Among her most recent works are *The Sphinx At Dawn* (published by The Seabury Press), *A Severed Wasp* (published by Farrar, Straus & Giroux), and the texts for two choral pieces published by Carl Fischer, Inc.

STARR LUTERI writes that she holds a Certificate of Merit for running up the highest bill on the church xerox machine—her sole award to date. When she isn't busy copying things, she is a "loving wife" (to David Hicks, who is the manager of the Logos Bookstore in Cincinnati, where they live), a "perfect mother" (to Suzanna and Peter), "an immaculate housekeeper and a poor speller." She is also a hard-working and self-critical writer.

Starr was born in 1951 in Geneva, New York, and later attended Western College, Miami University, and Cedarville College, from which she graduated with a B.A. in Christian Education. In addition to writing and raising her family, she finds time to quilt, cross-stitch, garden, and decorate eggs in the old Hungarian style, which requires a steady hand and almost infinite patience, and which uses hot wax, a stylus, and cold-water dyes. She does this, as she says, tongue firmly in cheek, "to occupy all those long, empty hours!"

"Ceyx" is her first published story.

Starr Luteri quotes Richard Adams from his introduction to *Unbroken Web*: "Dreams are the individual's folk-tales, and folk-tales are collective dreams."

CALVIN MILLER has been the pastor of the Westside Baptist Church in Omaha, Nebraska, for sixteen years. He was born in Oklahoma in 1936, graduated from high school in the town where he was born, and then attended Oklahoma Baptist University, from which he graduated in 1958 with a Bachelor of Science degree. He married Barbara Joyce Harmon the next year and later went on to Midwestern Theological Seminary, graduating with a Master of Divinity in 1962. His marriage was blessed with a daughter, Melanie Dawn, and a son, Timothy Grant, and he returned to Baptist Theological Seminary for his Doctor of Ministry, which he received in 1975.

Dr. Miller has written over fourteen books of popular theology and inspiration, which have included *Poems of Protest and Faith*, *That Elusive Thing Called Joy*, the well-loved "Singer" trilogy, and, recently, *The Valiant Papers*, *The Philippian Fragment*, and *The Guardians of Singreale*. Along the way, *Campus Life* magazine awarded him the Book of the Year Award in Fiction for *The Singer* (in 1975) and the Editor's Choice, Book of the Year Award for Fiction in 1982. He was also named the Midwestern Seminary Alumnus of the Year in 1981. In addition to his books, he has written poetry and free-lance articles which have been used in such journals as *Christianity Today* and *Young Life*.

He writes, "I am an avid raquetball player and I once had an open tennis tournament named after me where the trophy was a bronzed tennis shoe of mine. I am an artist whose painting was once used on *Short Horn Country*, which is a livestock breeder's journal." Dr. Miller believes strongly in the immediate and prime importance of evangelism in the church in this and every age. He has devoted his life to being an apologist who helps the church provide answers for the questions of a secular age. He encapsulates his "rule for life" in four words: "Time is a gift."

MARY MCDERMOTT SHIDELER was born and brought up in Topeka, Kansas. Following high school, she attended Swarthmore College, from which she graduated in 1938 with high honors, having majored in psychology and minored in philosophy and zoology. Since then she has continued to travel, lecture, and study all over the world, including periods in England, France, Germany, Japan, and India, as well as at Pendle Hill and at the Chicago Theological Seminary, which awarded her the Doctor of Divinity, *honoris causa*, in 1971.

She has produced an enormous body of work which includes *The Theology of Romatic Love* (a study of Charles Williams' writings); *Charles Williams, A Creed for a Christian Sceptic* (an Episcopal Book Club selection in 1968); *Consciousness of Battle* (a Religious Book Club selection in 1970); and the book of fables from which "Mother and the Flying Saucer" is taken. She has written introductions to *Are Women Human?* by Dorothy Sayers and *Taliessin through Logres, The Region of the Summer Stars,* and *Arthurian Torso* by Charles Williams and C. S. Lewis; and has published articles on Charles Williams and George MacDonald, as well as on topics as wide-ranging as the terminally ill, mysticism, fairy tales, and divorce. In addition, she reviews books for such publications as *Religion in Life, Theology Today, The New Review of Books and Religion,* and *The Christian Century.* She is also associated with such groups as the American Theological Society (Midwest Division), of which she is past president, and The Society for Descriptive Psychology, of which she has also been president.

In spite of a life of research and writing, she does not spend hours delving through the card files of a university library. She lives, in her words, "high in the foothills of the Rocky Mountains" where she can see the Continental Divide from her writing desk. At night the stars are incredibly clear, and by day she is surrounded by deep silence except for the sounds of the wind and the occasional barking of her two Great Pyrenees dogs, Beorna and Bianca.

A few years ago she fulfilled a long-unsatisfied desire and bought a folk harp. She found a teacher in the Boulder area and has been happily plucking and strumming since. She tells this story delightfully in an article called *Mary Had a Little Harp* printed in *The Folk Harp Journal.*

She is currently writing a book which is tentatively entitled *Persons, Behavior, and Worlds: The Descriptive Psychology Approach,* an introduction to the conceptual system developed by Dr. Peter Ossorio of the University of Colorado.